"   ivilege of being friends with
Rick McKinley, one of our country's greatest pastors. In the
current chaos of this experiment called American democracy,
Rick offers some of his best wisdom on how to speak truth
in love, how to be prophetic and pastoral, and how to challenge evil without becoming evil. We need this book now
more than ever."

Shane Claiborne, founder, The Simple Way; convener, Red
Letter Christians; activist; author, *Beating Guns*

"Apart from the Civil War in the nineteenth century and
the Civil Rights movement of the sixties, it's hard to name
a time when America has been so anxious and divided . . .
and the church is leading the charge. In this timely book,
Rick helps us discern the spirit of the age and faithfully
negotiate an increasingly jingoistic, angry, and divisive social context."

Alan Hirsch, award-winning author of numerous books
on leadership, organization, and spirituality

"*Faith for This Moment* will challenge and equip you as we
seek to live like Jesus—for such a time as this. Boldly questioning what it means to be the people of God right now—
Rick's words will light a fire in your soul. Quite simply: we
cannot afford to miss this book."

Ann Voskamp, *New York Times* bestselling author, *The
Broken Way* and *One Thousand Gifts*

"There can be few messages more urgent and exciting in our
world today than the fact that Jesus Christ is in the business of reconciliation. I'm so grateful to Rick McKinley for
distilling decades of experience as a pioneering pastor in
one of the least-churched cities in America into this timely
book. With his usual blend of intelligence and warmth, he

offers us a reason and a way to live with greater hope, grace, and beauty."

Pete Greig, founder, 24-7 Prayer International; senior pastor, Emmaus Rd, Guildford, UK

"In *Faith for This Moment*, Rick prophetically and practically calls us back to 'Church.' To be it, to love it, and to extend it to a world that is asking us to show them Jesus without all the religious trappings."

Hugh Halter, author, *Tangible Kingdom*, *FLESH*, and *Happy Hour*

"In *Faith for This Moment*, the caricature that has become known as Christianity is stripped away to reveal what it means to follow Jesus faithfully in this cultural moment. Rick encourages followers of Jesus to return to our deepest identity—children of God—and live as an alternative community in the midst of world that is as polarized as ever. If this is what being a Christian looks like in the future, then the world will take note."

AJ Swoboda, PhD; pastor; author, *Subversive Sabbath* and *Redeeming How We Talk*

"Brilliantly insightful and yet delivered with pastoral care. *Faith for This Moment* not only pinpoints the cultural tensions we all feel but gives us a hope-filled biblical framework to faithfully walk forward as Christians. This book is a huge win for the church today."

Chuck Bomar, pastor, Colossae Church in Portland, OR; author, *Serving Local Schools: Bring Christ's Compassion to the Core of YourCommunity*

"In our polarized culture, how are we to live faithfully to Jesus? *Faith for This Moment* reclaims exile as a powerful biblical theme, one that moves us beyond attempts to baptize the culture or burn it. Instead, McKinley offers constructive practices, 'rhythms of grace' as he calls them, that make us a distinct people who bear a beauty that blesses the world, the marks of our coming King."

Joshua Ryan Butler, pastor, Imago Dei Community; author, *The Pursuing God* and *The Skeletons in God's Closet*

"*Faith for This Moment* is a title that captures the heart-cry of many who are dizzy and confused about how to live an authentic Christian life in the midst of a rapidly changing and multifaceted world. In this short, accessible book, Rick McKinley does what he does best by replacing formula with faith and calling believers to radical discipleship rather than retreat. For anyone looking for a book that both names the unique cultural experience of Christians today while also providing honest biblical ways forward, this book will be like water to your soul."

Ken Wytsma, lead pastor, Village in Beaverton, Oregon; author, *The Myth of Equality* and *Redeeming How We Talk*

"*Faith for This Moment* is a book for this moment. In our world today, Christians are often categorized by cultural- and agenda-based forms of Christianity. Rick guides us back to Scripturally based vintage Christianity, and you will find yourself being encouraged, feeling like you aren't alone, and inspired to make a difference again for Jesus in our world. Every day it feels more embarrassing and confusing to say you are a Christian in today's world. Instead of having to either compromise truth or hiding our faith, Rick McKinley guides us into bold confidence of how to live out our faith more than ever in our towns and cities. If you are a Christian and you don't fit the cultural categories that are lately defining us, *Faith for This Moment* will be fresh wind for your heart and soul."

Dan Kimball, mission and leadership pastor, Vintage Faith Church; author, *Adventures in Churchland: Finding Jesus in the Mess of Organized Religion* and *They Like Jesus but Not the Church: Insights from Emerging Generations*

"The church exists today in a cultural flux of unfamiliar change and transition. The strangeness of the moment can leave churches and followers of Jesus scratching their heads and searching their souls in an effort to figure out what to do. In this book Rick shows us that this new space is not so new—people of faith have passed this way before. He masterfully shows us how we can use classical practices, with God's help, to be the Jesus's church in today's culture. His book is a much-needed compass."

Mark Strong, pastor; author; founder, Father-Shift Conference

"*Faith for This Moment* is a must-read for any follower of Jesus, regardless of political beliefs or socioeconomic status. It proves itself as a thorough road map of the shifting cultural landscape. Read this book!"

Albert Tate, senior pastor, Fellowship Monrovia

"Rick is one of the best leaders, smartest thinkers, and most insightful teachers I know. In *Faith for This Moment*, he brings all of that, plus years of experience church planting in a post-Christian city, to bear on our cultural moment. I found myself furiously taking notes in between ah-ha moments of insight. This book is a manual for the church in the post-Christian world."

John Mark Comer, pastor of teaching and vision, Bridgetown Church; author, *God Has a Name* and *Loveology: God. Love. Marriage. Sex. And the Never-Ending Story of Male and Female.*

FAITH
FOR THIS
MOMENT

FAITH
FOR THIS
MOMENT

**NAVIGATING A POLARIZED WORLD
AS THE PEOPLE OF GOD**

RICK McKINLEY

BakerBooks
a division of Baker Publishing Group
Grand Rapids, Michigan

Published by Baker Books
a division of Baker Publishing Group
PO Box 6287, Grand Rapids, MI 49516-6287
www.bakerbooks.com

Printed in the United States of America

Library of Congress Cataloging-in-Publication Data
Names: McKinley, Rick, author.
Title: Faith for this moment : navigating a polarized world as the people of God / Rick McKinley.
Description: Grand Rapids, MI : Baker Books, a division of Baker Publishing Group, [2018] | Includes bibliographical references.
Identifiers: LCCN 2018007044 | ISBN 9780801015588 (pbk.)
Subjects: LCSH: Christianity and culture. | Christian life.
Classification: LCC BR115.C8 M2655 2018 | DDC 261.0973—dc23
LC record available at https://lccn.loc.gov/2018007044

Author is represented by ChristopherFerebee.com, Attorney and Literary Agent.

18 19 20 21 22 23 24   7 6 5 4 3 2 1

To Jeff Marsh
As we have stood together
since the first day
of the Imago Dei Community,
your faithfulness has been an anchor
through many storms.

CONTENTS

INTRODUCTION

This book is the culmination of several years of pastoring in the lovely city of Portland, Oregon. Portland is proudly progressive and considered highly unchurched. The blessing of this place is seen in the beauty of Oregon's geography. The snow-peaked Mount Hood looks out over our city like a watchman on a wall as the Willamette and Columbia Rivers flow around us.

There is another beauty within our city, and it is a thriving community of Jesus followers from all stripes and traditions. We are learning how to love our neighbors and serve our city together, not as one church but as "the" church. Within that beauty, however, are large challenges that loom over us. Followers of Jesus are a minority community in Portland, and Portland itself has a strong culture that powerfully shapes how people think and act. One significant challenge is how to be faithful to Jesus when the culture around us has no place for our faith.

The theme of exile came to me from reading many Old Testament theologians. Most prominent was Walter Brueggemann, whose poetic insight into the prophets and ability to see our own local and national challenges in light of Scripture helped me to understand exile as an extremely useful and hopeful metaphor that can frame our understanding of what it means to be the people of God now.

For all its beauty, Portland has become a microcosm of the broader culture. The polarizing categories that divide our nation are amplified in Portland. The daily shouting at one another from our echo chambers has created a lack of the civility required to move forward together as a community. The people of God have an opportunity in the midst of our cultural moment to create civility in the public square. We are called by God to love our neighbor and our enemy, to embrace rather than demonize those whom we disagree with. While Portland appears polarized, there are beachheads of unlikely partners working together for the common good on some of our city's hardest problems. Like many American cities, Portland has several crisis points: an overloaded foster care system, homelessness, and sex trafficking, to name a few. Yet in these spaces, we are discovering a way to embrace one another, listen to each other with empathetic ears, and actually move forward together to create solutions. We are learning how to build up, not simply tear down. In the pages that follow, I will explain a way of being the people of God in this moment that, if taken seriously, can lead us into a type of citizenship that is faithful to Jesus and a blessing to our local communities. In a moment like ours, the church—if we are faithful to Christ—can be a force for healing and hope.

Ours is a hurting world, and our country is fractured and polarized, but God has chosen this time and place for us to live out our faith and faithfulness. That is no accident.

What I hope to do in the following pages is to provide a framework for understanding the moment in which we are living and to help us see within that moment the possibilities God has for us.

In the first few chapters of this book, I will introduce the theme of exile and explain why I think it is both helpful and powerful for understanding where we fit in society today and how we fit best into that society.

In the second half, I will introduce you to spiritual practices that I believe have a threefold power for those who practice them. The practices that I propose have the power to transform us personally in a way that leads to faithfulness to Jesus. They also have the power to preserve our identity as followers of Jesus in a culture whose powers of assimilation are at work on us every day. Finally, these practices have the power to be both a blessing and a witness to our neighbors, communities, and nation. I realize this sounds like a huge oversell of these practices, but in reality, they are simply ways in which we have been called by Jesus to live our lives. Our homes, our work, our money, and our worship create the shape of our lives as individuals, families, churches, and communities. When we enter into these practices, we enter into rhythms of God's grace that lead us to life as he means for us to experience it.

My prayer is that together we will discover what it means to be the people of God now, right here in our fractured moment, and that with this discovery we will become the salt and light the world so desperately needs.

ONE

The Moment

I turned on the radio. It was about eight o'clock in the morning on Sunday, June 12, 2016. My drive into the city was the same as most Sundays at eight in the morning: empty sidewalks and no traffic. NPR was reporting on a shooting that had occurred in the early morning hours at a nightclub in Orlando. The facts were just emerging on my drive in, but in the hours and days that followed, details would come to light revealing that this was an event of mass proportion.

Omar Mateen walked into the Pulse nightclub and in a savage attack killed forty-nine people and wounded fifty-eight others. The Pulse was a gay nightclub, it was Latin night, and most of the victims were Latino. Mateen reportedly frequented the club, though the FBI and the CIA found no evidence of this. On his 911 call, Mateen swore allegiance to the leader of the Islamic State of Iraq, Abu Bakr al-Baghdadi.

The shooting became one of the deadliest mass shootings in US history, the deadliest terrorist attack since September 11,

2001, the deadliest incident of violence against the LGBTQ community, and an unspeakable act of violence against Latin American people. Mateen told a negotiator that his actions were retaliation for the American-led interventions in Iraq and Syria.

At church we held a moment of silence for the victims and their families, though the details were still sketchy. In the early hours of Sunday, June 12, so many facets of American society collided in an act of horrendous evil: sexuality, racism, gun control, Islamic fundamentalism, and a global war on terror that was proving to be incredibly complex with victory almost impossible to define. In our moment of silence, a fog filled my head. How would those families recover? What were our gay friends and neighbors thinking and feeling right now? Why? How? What the . . . ?

How do people who follow Jesus respond in moments like this?

Driving home from church, my radio still tuned to NPR, I listened to an interview of a local pastor in Orlando. The reporter summarized the tension with poignancy and firmness in one profound question: "How do evangelicals respond to this crisis when it is very clear politically that evangelicals are antigay and pro-gun?" That question rocked me. The pastor was stumped. I wondered how I would answer the reporter if she were to ask me the same question.

The gospel that was meant to be good news for all people was being translated by this reporter for American society, communicating that followers of Jesus were somehow aligned with the shooter's beliefs. While not suggesting that Christians are pro-murder, this journalist was unearthing what no one wants to talk about: essentially, that it is hard for

Christians to show compassion to victims and families of the Orlando nightclub shooting when certain streams within the church have sent the wrong message to the culture around us. What the reporter had heard the church communicate was that Mateen had the right to bear arms and that his denouncement of the LGBTQ community was compatible with the right way to think and vote. She assumed that this is the way Jesus's followers think and vote. While I felt the pushback internally, I had to admit that this is how Christians are widely perceived.

Her point was made on me, and I could imagine countless people who don't follow Jesus nodding their heads along with her. Now when we should be declaring, "The God of all comfort is full of mercy," our voices are muted because our society has heard, "Our God likes guns and hates gay people." This is a biblical and theological misrepresentation, but it is hard to put the toothpaste back in the tube once it's out.

Sixteen months later Donald Trump became our forty-fifth president. The election was one of the most divisive in the last fifty years, and depending on where you live, it may have left you dumbfounded, as it did the newscasters who were reporting on the election. Most channels showed men and women at a loss for words, and yet clearly a good portion of the country had voted for Trump. The next morning it seemed as if the moderate voices had been raptured overnight, and our country was split like a great chasm, right down the middle. Reports showed that 80 percent of evangelicals had voted for Trump. The question the NPR reporter had asked that pastor in Orlando came flooding back to me.

Now What?

This book is not about how a Christian should vote. I believe that Christians should vote, and they should vote their consciences. I am not writing to endorse a candidate or a political party. I am asking myself and you as well, What is the church as a whole telling the world about Jesus? This seems like an impossible question to answer, because there is a vast spectrum of churches filled with a multitude of opinions concerning theology and social issues. Who are we even talking about when we talk about the people of God?

The spectrum of churches contains many denominations and theological traditions, and some, if not most, would not be happy to be associated with the others. But a spectrum of theological views and social opinions exists for a reason, each group believing it is closer to the intentions of Christ and the application of Scripture than the others.

To the world at large, this spectrum is very confusing. Most people who don't follow Jesus or attend church are unaware of how detailed and complex our differences are. The watching world often lumps us together into one group. This means that telling someone we believe in and follow Jesus may bring to their mind Appalachian snake handlers; the militant, antigay hate speech of Westboro Baptist; an experience they had with a Southern Baptist; or a preacher they saw on TV. They may think we speak in tongues and shake on the ground, or they may think we despise scientific knowledge and reject evolution.

Sadly, few would think that we are rational people with a deep and abiding sense of the grace of Jesus and that we possess the heart and the will to love and serve the world in his name. The fact is that the loudest and strangest beliefs and practices on the spectrum make the news, while hundreds of thousands of believers who are actually living as salt and light in the world do not make the prime-time news shows or go viral on the web.

The world around us is not aware of the intricacies of theological debate, and the lack of unity in the church continues to cause confusion for those on the outside looking in.

The moment in which we live is not cut-and-dry. There are no easy answers to the problems of the world, and bumper-sticker opinions won't solve the deep-seated issues that we face. Sexuality, racism, immigration, terror, religion, war, wealth and poverty, truth and lies are all on the table now, and we can't assume that having the right political stripe will make everything clear. We are a society that is messy and complicated, and it appears that Christians, whose voices have been drowned out by misrepresentation and misunderstanding, have little to say about the things that matter most to the world.

Many people who follow Jesus protest the statistics, insisting that not all Christians vote or think like the stereotypes. But if we are being honest, we would admit that Christians who stand on the other side of the fence are guilty of similar compromises on different issues. You may be against building a wall along the border of Mexico, but are you willing to fight for the rights of the unborn? Where does someone go who doesn't fit into the given political and social boxes? What do you do if you are serious about your faith in Jesus but feel more and more that the speech and actions being used by certain Christians don't accurately reflect what you believe?

The question that keeps gnawing at me and that I am desperate to try to answer is this: What does it mean to be the people of God now? That's the question that drives this book. What I am excited about is this: we are not unique in this moment; God's people have been in moments like ours. They have survived times of being marginalized and misunderstood. They have come through times when they were disciplined by God for unfaithfulness and found redemption in his mercy. Most encouraging is that, throughout history, God's people have found a way to be faithful, prophetic, and imaginative as they discovered fresh ways to announce that Jesus is still Lord of all things, even in moments like this.

Christians are facing a crisis right now. The crisis comes from a sense of loss in three distinct areas: identity, place, and practice.

The Loss of Identity

Once upon a time in America, the majority of the population shared Judeo-Christian values. The average American was somewhat familiar with the biblical faith in Jesus and more than likely had attended some type of Christian church at some point in their life. Society held to values that today we call traditional, that aligned somewhat with what Christians at the time considered biblical norms. It appeared that God, and specifically the God of the Bible, was blessing America.

Back then people who followed Jesus had an identity that fit well within American society. Pastors were respected, church attendance was far greater than it is today, and debates in the public square took into consideration what God or the church had to say on the matter. That day has long since passed. For followers of Jesus, our identity within the culture has become marginalized as society has grown more pluralistic and secular. Today hundreds of beliefs and worldviews compete for the attention of the hearts and minds of people.

This plurality of voices and opinions has marginalized the voice of faith at best and shown disdain for it at worst. The ethics of Judeo-Christian America have been replaced with the ethics of generic spirituality, which demands only that we be nice to other people and allow them to do whatever they want. In the world of pluralism, Jesus's claim to be the exclusive way to the Father doesn't come off as good news but instead sounds oppressive and arrogant. Which means that a young person in an urban center today feels more apologetic than proud for being a Christian.

Christians who once felt their faith had a home in America are realizing that they are increasingly a minority group. This is especially true for white Christians. The African American church and other churches of color have a long history of living out their faith while being marginalized by the majority culture. For white Christians, not fitting in and being marginalized is an entirely new experience and has led to a loss of identity within the culture.

The Loss of Place

The loss of identity leads to the second loss: the loss of place. Christian voices have receded to the margins within society, and this marginalization has been growing for several decades. The loss of place creates uneasiness, particularly for white evangelicals, whose privilege within society is being threatened for the first time in their religious memory. This uneasiness has led many to scramble for security, running to politics to seek salvation.

To try to maintain Christian values, Christian politicians and political organizations have created bills, hoping to exclude the people and the things that threaten to destabilize their ways of being Americans. The goal is to prevent ideas and practices that are unfamiliar to them and to preserve the ones in which they find security. From gay marriage to gun control, these efforts have all but backfired. In seeking to retain a voice within society and to hold on to a place in the public square, Christians have tried to retain a beachhead in the perceived war against them. But the beach has eroded, and it appears that political and cultural power has eroded with it. The lingering result of the culture wars is the lasting impression that Christians, and particularly evangelical Christians, are more of a political party than a movement of believers committed to following Jesus and sharing his gospel.

Christians who are embarrassed to admit to the designation are not ashamed of Jesus but are afraid that their peers will assume that following Jesus requires them to join the political forces that seem to speak for Jesus in ways that Jesus himself never spoke. The result is Christians who love Jesus but find themselves confused by who they are now and where their place in society might be.

The Loss of Practice

The last loss Christians are facing is the loss of practice. They no longer understand what it means to practice their faith.

This came home to me a few years ago while I was driving down a street in downtown Portland. A Muslim man with a long beard was standing at a bus stop with two young children. He wore a prayer cap and a long tunic, his daughter's head was covered with a hijab, and his son was dressed like him. He was standing in the middle of hipster central dressed as if he were going for tea in Afghanistan. What struck me was how clear it was that he was practicing his faith. His dress, as a visible symbol of his faith, laid out for himself and displayed for others when he worshiped, how he worshiped, the words he prayed, and the exact time he prayed them.

By contrast, the faith I was introduced into when I was eighteen was primarily a private experience. I did most of my praying and reading by myself. Outside of Sunday worship there was a Bible study or a service project or some door knocking to do, but no clear path existed concerning what these practices were supposed to look like. Rather than instructing me in how to pray, read Scripture, and love my neighbor, the pastors seemed primarily concerned with my sex life and how much alcohol I was consuming. I learned what not to do but not really what I was supposed to do.

Practicing the Christian faith in public and in private can mean everything and nothing to some extent. Such practice can be anything from picketing an abortion clinic to voting for a candidate to having a quiet time. Because there is such a wide spectrum of belief, anything goes. Ironically, Christian practice tends to get reduced to being nice, not bothering anyone, and not taking the faith too seriously or causing a scene. The radical, cross-bearing faith of Peter, James, and John is inspiring to read about but seemingly impossible to replicate.

The problem as I see it is that, for most Christians, their current practice does not distinguish them from the greater society, nor does it necessarily form them to be salt and light in the world. Many Christians don't really know what it means to practice their faith today.

Who Should We Blame?

As a result of these losses, Christians across the wide spectrum of belief are increasingly finding it difficult to answer the question, What does it mean to be the people of God now? As with any loss, the losses Christians are experiencing are disorienting. Questions arise on how to remedy the situation, but answers are difficult to find. Almost all seek first to blame, pointing fingers at the culture at large or portions of the faith community in which they live. Liberals blame conservatives, and conservatives blame liberals. People often find it far easier to fight over issues they disagree on than to hear the demands of the gospel concerning how they should spend their time and their money and whom they should invite to their tables. When blaming dies down, people may make a grab for power, seeking to regain the influence they once had. In grabbing for some sort of stabilizing security, however, they end up empty-handed. The efforts to reconstruct their former way of life fail.

The divisions caused by liberal and conservative agendas are not the only explanation for this failure. The failure has come from something far more serious for all Christ followers, liberal and conservative. Because we have all marinated in American culture for so long, we have become enculturated. We have grown comfortable with the cultural air that we breathe and have been radically affected by it. We are all consumers, we are all shaped by the desire for affluence, we are all highly connected to the technology that both entertains us and shapes the narrative of our lives, and we all depend on national security and class divides to protect our way of life. These aspects of life are not tied to any biblical doctrine we believe or church we attend. We are swimming in the stream of culture, shaped by the same realities as everyone else, and rarely if ever do we stop to question our participation in this way of life. Therefore, on the one hand, we Christians are increasingly being marginalized by society for our beliefs. On the other hand, we are simultaneously becoming more and more enculturated by the forces of American society so that we are no different from the rest of society in many ways.

These forces appear to affect everyone on the wide spectrum of Christian belief, from liberal, progressive Christians to more conservative believers. Enculturation is a by-product of living in American society. No one is exempt from the forces of American culture, and as a result, the claims of Christ and his gospel have been drowned out by the white noise of buying more stuff, making more money, consuming more information and entertainment, and following the twenty-four-hour news cycles that tell us if it's safe to go outside.

The speed at which we can access all of the above is immediate, and there is no indication that things will slow down anytime soon. The greatest threat that we Christians face is not the rejection of our values and beliefs in the public square but our own participation in the stream of culture that shapes our identity more powerfully than our faith in Jesus does. Faith becomes one more thing that people consume in a long list of purchases that we hope will make up a meaningful life. The privatization of faith and the marginalization of its purposes in our public lives are evidence that we have lost our deepest identity and compromised our strongest allegiance. Hardly any of this has taken place as an act of defiant rebellion. Slowly and over time, we have passively forgotten the story of which we are a part, our identity as the people of God, and the way of life we have been called to live that runs counter to the aspirations of the empire. So what do we do?

Denial and Despair

How we respond in this moment will shape what our faith will look like in this new world. Denial may be how many of us will respond. Dismissing the facts and denying the realities, we can just keep going on the way we are. But if we do, we will find that we have lost a lot more than religious liberty. Our very souls are at stake. If we hide from the world, we are removing ourselves from the very people Jesus has called us to love in his name.

Another way to respond is to despair. We can close the curtains and bury our noses in the book of Revelation and wait for the rapture to come and take us home. While I don't deny that Jesus is going to come back and bring his kingdom with him, he never gives us the option of hiding from the world and waiting to be transported off the planet. If we choose despair, we will miss the beauty and redemption that he is bringing into the world—even this world and even in the shape that it is in.

A New Possibility

A final option, and one we will explore in this book, is that we can see the possibilities God has for us. When we remember our story, we recognize that the people of God have been here before, and they found their God faithful. We are not alone in our marginal moment. In seeing these possibilities, we can grab hold of the hope that Jesus is still King over all things.

This hope is not without cost. It will require that we rediscover ancient practices that sustained God's people in conditions like our own. It will demand that we turn from the small gods we have come to depend on for our comfort, security, and identity and turn back to the living God who has bought us with the blood of his beloved Son. Along the way, we will need to imagine new and fresh ways of expressing faithfulness to Jesus, love to our neighbors, and allegiance to the King of heaven and earth who is present in sustaining ways through his Spirit.

This is not the time to be in denial or to give in to despair. This is the time to hope in new possibilities. It is the time to remember that our God has preserved his people throughout history and will do so now as well. The God of the past is the God of the present, and he invites us to discover in new ways what it means to be the people of God now.

The Idea of Exile

God's people throughout history often found themselves in times and places that were hostile to their faith. They survived moments within history when they were marginalized at best and persecuted at worst. There were also times when

God's people found themselves in powerful cultures, such as that of Babylon, whose wealth and power threatened to enculturate them and turn them away from faithfulness and toward apathy and idolatry. These moments were known as exile.

Exile in Scripture is both a historical reality for the people of Israel in the Old Testament and a metaphor used by New Testament writers to help Christians understand how to faithfully follow Jesus in inhospitable times and places. In this book, I will be arguing that exile is an important way for Christians to understand what it means to be the people of God now. We will discover from the past how to be faithful in the present. Exile is a way of getting our minds and our hearts around understanding how to be faithful to Jesus in the current cultural moment in which we live.

Jesus asks us one thing: Will we be faithful to him as he has been faithful to us? We are all broken and sinful in deep places within us, and we will never follow Jesus perfectly, but I am convinced that there is a deeper faithfulness we can discover. There is a way of living by faith that allows us to be distinct in our world, transformed by our King, and a blessing to all people as we announce the good news that Jesus is Lord of all. At the end of the day, when we stand before Jesus, faithfulness to him and his Word is really the only thing we will answer for. As we look back to the past and see God's faithfulness to his people in exile and the people's response to their God, it is my prayer that we will find a way to be faithful to Jesus in our moment of exile.

In the following chapters, we will travel back in time to understand what exile meant for the people of God in the Old Testament, and we will discover what exile means for us today. Then we will look at ways to practice our faith that will lead us to faithfulness to Christ and will preserve our identity in Jesus as we live inside our culture and bear witness to the world around us that Jesus truly is the way, the truth, and the life.

TWO

Where in the World Is Exile?

Imagine waking up one morning, and as you look outside, you find that you're in an entirely different country. The street signs are illegible to you; the way the people are dressed and the language they speak are completely foreign to you. Even the houses are built differently. Over the next few days, you venture outside. You can't understand a word anyone is saying, and no one is particularly excited to talk to you anyway. You stand out in every crowd like a flashing neon sign.

As you try to acclimate to this new place, you realize that if you can find a church that worships Jesus, then you should be able to find some help and hospitality from your brothers and sisters in the faith. You scour the streets and find someone who speaks your language, but as you explain that you are looking for a church, you are met with a look of confusion. This person has never heard of a church, and they explain that the worship

of the people of this place doesn't involve Jesus or anything that you would relate to. Everything has changed. Everything that you once knew, relied on, and found familiar is gone.

If I were to sum up the last chapter, I would put it this way: the way previous generations in the church understood their place in society is gone, and what life is going to look like for believers in the future must be thought through in a new way. Why? Because the traditional social structures that once validated the church's way of life are no more.

Exile Defined

What is hopeful, however, is that these conditions are exactly the same conditions in which most people in Scripture found themselves. The term that best describes this situation is *exile*. Here is a partial definition: "Exile was a period when the promises of the past and the shape of the future had to be evaluated in terms of a new experience without the traditional self-validating structures, such as the monarchy and the state, the temple and the institutional cult."[1]

Essentially, what we find in the Old Testament as well as in the New is that the people of God often found themselves grieving the loss of their identity as they once understood it, their place in the broader society, and their practices of worship. But God continued to be present among them. His presence and relentless pursuit of his people caused them to discover that they had been given a new identity in a new place and a new set of practices to know him in deeper and more intimate ways. This all happened in exile.

A brief overview will help us see that the theme of exile runs throughout the Bible.

Our Rich History in Exile as the People of God

Adam and Eve

Removal from the Garden of Eden was humanity's first and worst exile. After Adam and Eve sinned, God removed them from the garden. They lost their innocence and much more. They also lost their identity as God's children who walked with God in the garden and stewarded his creation in a state of shalom, or harmony. This loss, as we all know, wreaked havoc for all of creation, including for you and me and our neighbors.

After Adam and Eve left the garden, life as they understood it was gone forever. They were not going back. The new place in which they found themselves was a completely different environment. Their place in the world of tending and stewarding creation was no longer a fruitful, luscious garden. Now the dirt was hard and the thorns were thick. This new place was a mere shadow of the former one.

Finally, the way in which they worshiped God was forever changed. They lost access to him. Their method of just being with him was now blocked off.

In the first three chapters, Scripture sets the stage for the divine drama with a detailed account of humanity's exile. We are left wondering how the drama will play out. And we are left with the question, How will return ever be made possible?

Abram and Sarai

With Abram and Sarai, the theme of exile continued. Abram was called by God to leave his family and his country and to go to the place God would show him. Abram and his wife, Sarai, set out to leave their family, friends, and the land they had called home for most of their lives. They didn't know where they were going, and all they really had was faith in the God who had told them to leave.

The title that the book of Hebrews gives to these two exiles is "strangers and wanderers." Think about the word *strangers*. Our identity is made up of many things, but most important is being known. We live in community with other people. We are called into our identity through families and friends. All of that was gone now for Abram and Sarai. The identity they would be known by now was stranger—someone who is not a part of us.

We don't know a lot about their lives in Ur of the Chaldeans other than their family was wealthy, having servants and livestock and all that comes with wealth. The house they had called home was replaced by a tent, and everyone and everything that belonged to Abram and Sarai was now on the move. They didn't even have a destination—only the call to leave and go. They would have to wait on God to let them know where they were going. The loss of place was significant, but the call of God was greater.

We are also told that Abram's family members were pagan worshipers. Abram's father, Terah, did not worship the God who spoke to Abram by name. The worship that Abram had been raised on, the rituals he was familiar with, and the way in which he thought about faith and truth and life and death were all about to change. The ways of his father would not be his ways, and so Abram lost his gods and the worship that he understood they required.

Exile is about loss. We would be shortsighted to think that Abram and Sarai didn't grieve all their losses. To lose our sense of identity, the familiarity of place, and the faith of our fathers is to suffer a big loss. But God did not simply take away; he also gave.

In the call of Abram, we read:

> The LORD had said to Abram, "Go from your country, your people and your father's household to the land I will show you.
>> "I will make you into a great nation,
>>> and I will bless you;
>> I will make your name great,
>>> and you will be a blessing.
>> I will bless those who bless you,
>>> and whoever curses you I will curse;
>> and all peoples on earth
>>> will be blessed through you." (Gen. 12:1–3)

The Lord's call of Abram into exile away from his former identity, place, and practice of worship was a call toward something new, something that all of us have benefited from. If you are a follower of Jesus, you have received that blessing through the seed of Abraham, Jesus. This shows us that while exile is a place of loss, it is also a place of hope, because the God who is sovereign over the times in which we live is the one who sustains us in exile.

Abram and Sarai were given new identities: Abraham and Sarah. They were taken into a new land that would be known as the Promised Land. God gave that land to Abraham and Sarah and to their descendants. God also gave them something they never thought possible. He gave them a son, Isaac. He also gave them a new way of practicing faith. They would be God's friends and the father and mother of an entire nation from which Christ would come. It turns out that exile was the first step in a story of hope.

Joseph

The theme of exile continued with the story of Joseph. Joseph was exiled from his family and his home and ended up in Egypt. Over the years, he rose in status from a prisoner in a jail cell to the second in command in all of Egypt. Joseph lost his identity, his home (place), and his way of life (practice), but God was working behind the scenes, and no one saw it until things got bad.

God revealed to Joseph through Pharaoh's dream that a famine would take over the entire land. Because of Joseph's leadership, Egypt prepared and stored plenty of food during years of abundance so they would be ready for the famine. No one else did. In this new world in which Joseph found himself, he became the person who would save thousands of people. He was given a new name, a new home, and a new role in Pharaoh's empire. Through these new surroundings and an unfamiliar way of life in Egypt, Joseph and all of Israel (and Egypt for that matter) were saved by God through exile. We hear the echoes of this salvation in the words of Joseph after he was reunited with his family in Egypt: "You intended to harm me, but God intended it for good to accomplish what is now being done, the saving of many lives" (Gen. 50:20).

The saving of many lives . . . If Joseph had not been exiled, lives would not have been saved. Before we despair too much about where believers fit in the world today, we need to consider what God might be doing. He just might be shaking things up to save many lives, ours included.

Moses and the Israelites

The theme of exile continued with Moses as he emancipated God's people from slavery. The Israelites' identity was that of slaves, their place was slavery in Egypt, and their practice of worship was seemingly lost. But God heard their cries and responded with salvation. Through Moses's leadership, God rescued his people after four hundred years of slavery in Egypt. With signs and wonders, the Israelites fled the oppressive imperial regime under which they had suffered the harsh conditions of forced servitude.

God's people experienced the joy of escaping Egypt and seeing God's miracle of parting the Red Sea. But this joy was short-lived. They found themselves displaced in the desert, wondering where they were and who they were supposed to be now. They were no longer slaves, but what did it mean to be free? They had no set practice of worshiping the God who called himself I Am Who I Am. What would worship look like, and what would it mean for their life together as a community?

The traditions of the past had been lost to them. They would need to rediscover who they were and where they were going and how to live in the world. The book of Exodus tells the story of the community formation of God's people. They were like many of us, and they weren't up for this level of reorientation. They quickly demanded to return to slavery rather than face the implications of what God had in mind for them. In the same way, many of us long for the past and the certainty we felt about the way things were "back then." We long to feel secure. We want the assurance of what we believed. The Israelites in the desert of Sinai similarly wanted to return to what was familiar, even if it meant a life of servitude. We should be cautious about our longing for the past. It is better to grieve our loss than to enslave ourselves trying to recover the past.

In the desert, God gave the Israelites a new identity. He called them his people: "For you are a people holy to the LORD your God. The LORD your God has chosen you out of all the peoples on the face of the earth to be his people, his treasured possession" (Deut. 7:6). In Egypt, they were slaves. In the exile of the desert wanderings, they learned they were God's treasured possession. They were being called to a new place, a place of promise that they had heard of through the stories of their fathers Abraham, Isaac, and Jacob. Stories about the promises of God that were spoken in the past were now going to shape their future.

Exile in the desert of Sinai created communal identity and communal hope. It was the place where they began to believe they were who God said they were and where they were called to put their sights on a new place, a place their sons and daughters would possess.

Most importantly, the desert was where the people of God developed a life of worship. We don't really know what worship looked like for them in Egypt. Many of the old customs might have been lost. We get a glimpse of this when Moses has no intention of circumcising his son. The angel of the Lord was preparing to kill him until Moses's wife stepped in and saved him by performing the circumcision herself. Moses didn't understand that the sign of the covenant God had made in the past was important in his moment. It is safe to assume, therefore, that the Israelites had grown apathetic in their worship.

But in the desert exile, all of that changed. In the desert, they built a tabernacle, ordained priests, entered into a covenant with Yahweh, and learned what it meant to love God and their neighbor. They also learned what it meant to repent of sin and offer sacrifices to God, what it meant to pray and worship him, and most importantly, what it meant to live with God in the midst of their life together. God was present by cloud and fire. In exile, the people's worship was formed and practiced, as it would be for thousands of years.

Exile, while full of threats, is also a place of imaginative worship where God dwells with his people in specificity. New practices are learned, new insights are gained into God's identity and character, and what it means to be his people is spelled out. The place we expect to be a place of desolation turns out to be a place of new creation, and God seems more than capable of making it so.

Are We Making Too Much of This?

One could argue that, in utilizing the theme of exile for understanding the situation of the church and Christ followers in twenty-first-century America, we are stretching the theme beyond where it is intended to go. As we prepare to turn to the primary understanding of exile in the Old Testament, the Babylonian exile, we must answer this question: Is it appropriate to use the theme of exile when talking about believers today? In other words, does Scripture give us permission to use the term to understand ourselves in our current situation?

To answer the question, we only need to turn to the book of First Peter. In his first letter, Peter wrote to believers who were scattered throughout Asia Minor. They had lost their identity, place, and familiar practices of life before Jesus Christ. Peter understood and used the theme of exile to help them get their footing in the new world they inhabited. Here is how he started his letter: "Peter, an apostle of Jesus Christ, to God's elect, exiles scattered throughout the provinces of Pontus, Galatia, Cappadocia, Asia and Bithynia" (1:1).

Peter referred to those he wrote in two ways: God's chosen people and the people of God who were exiles far from home. Peter used the theme of exile with its rich history in the Old Testament to help his readers understand their identity, their place, and the practices of a new life they had been given in Christ.

In this sense, all of God's people in all of the ages are exiles. This was the case before American Christians felt marginalized by society, and it will be the case after. Exile is the place where we live out our faith in Jesus.

We will return to First Peter in the chapters to come, but for now, it is important to note that exile can work as both a theme and a literal experience. For the Jews in the Old Testament, exile was their actual reality. It described their physical dislocation as they were carried off by a foreign power. In the New Testament, exile was used metaphorically to denote the way in which God's people were to understand their own displacement in the world. Through the power of Christ, God was making them into new creatures with a spiritual home that was not presently here but was coming with Christ. The same is true for us.

Exile helps us to understand what it meant to be the people of God throughout history in the hope that we will discover ways in which we can be the people of God in the present.

Exile helps us to understand our new identity, our new place in the world, and the new ways in which we can practice our faith in the moment in which we find ourselves.

Jesus the True Exile

Understanding the ways in which God's people discovered faithfulness in exile helps followers of Jesus today not fall into denial or despair about our current state. The reality is that Jesus, the one we worship, was an exile. The Son left the Father's side and went to a far country. Exiled into full humanity with the limitations of a human body, walking in the dusty steps of fallen creation, he lived among us a stranger, one who was rejected and despised. In doing so, he didn't fight for his heavenly rights or huddle away in a cave but boldly loved and served and preached about a kingdom of another world that he was bringing for all who felt cast out. He practiced a life of love and worship of his Father that people found unfamiliar but couldn't help being attracted to. His was a life of loving mercy and the tangible touch of grace. He called us and gave us a new name: beloved. The identity that he himself had with the Father was given to us. Displaced from heaven, he willingly took his place on the cross and was exiled to the grave. Conquering the grave, he rose to proclaim his triumph over all powers and authorities and little kingdoms that fill the world today.

This exile for Jesus was also the means by which he opened for us with his own blood a way to the Father through the Son by the Spirit. To follow him is to experience exile. We are to be in the world but not of it, as Jesus prayed in John 17. Because Jesus didn't fight the culture or hide away from it or fall into despair but instead preached a hope that surpassed exile and even death, we need to follow him into that hope. It is Jesus's hope that will carry us through exile. The difference for those of us experiencing exile on the other side of the cross is that our King has already defeated and overthrown the powers of sin and death that had taken us captive. His kingdom is breaking in and setting people free from the kingdom of darkness. Ours is an exile of victory, where we are empowered to live faithfully to our King from his own Spirit that indwells us as we fight the good fight of faith and await his kingdom to come in all of its fullness. We are invited to be hopeful exiles.

THREE

Babylon

My great-grandparents on my mom's side lived to be nearly a hundred years old. My great-grandma Yatchmenoff lived to be 104. Every Christmas starting when I was in sixth grade, my family would tell me to spend time with them because this could be their last Christmas with us. As things turned out, they would live to see my twins be born and would become great-great-grandparents, not passing away until I was in my midthirties. That is a lot of last Christmases.

I remember hearing their stories of growing up in the Bay Area, and at that time, their suburb of San Francisco was mostly orchards. I heard stories of how one girl in my great-grandmother's elementary school class rode a cow to school! I often thought about how much the world changed during their lifetimes. They lived from the time of the first automobiles to the technological revolution of the early 2000s. The world was constantly changing and advancing, and it also grew more and more unfamiliar to them in their later years.

The simple life they had lived as children was replaced by a world of endless gadgets that were too confusing for them to operate. Grandpa loved his TV though. He was happy about that advancement, and it helped him root on the Oakland A's until his last days.

My great-grandparents experienced radical change in the world during their lifetimes. In the closing decades of their lives, the world looked nothing like it had during their childhoods. In that sense, they were far from home. Yet in another sense, the changes they experienced brought blessings and made them feel at home in the world. In small ways, their experience was an experience of exile.

For God's people, that same "at-homeness" and "foreignness" of exile existed simultaneously. We looked at the theme of exile through the story line of Scripture. We now come to the most prominent exilic story in the Bible: the story of the southern kingdom of Israel in Babylon.[1] It is a story of great loss but also a story of great discovery—of a new identity, a new place, and new practices of worship. This exile would forever change the course of faith for the people of God.

Empire and Exile

Almost nine centuries after leaving Egypt and entering the Promised Land, the people of God experienced the judgment of God for their sin and wickedness. After David and Solomon, the kingdom of Israel split and cycled through various kings. Some did right in the sight of the Lord, but most did not. The northern kingdom was taken into captivity by the Assyrians. The southern kingdom (known as Judah) continued to exist, and King Josiah attempted a great reform to turn the hearts of the people back to God. But the people had sinned so greatly that God brought them into captivity in Babylon.

Enter Nebuchadnezzar. Nebuchadnezzar ruled for over forty years and was not only a conqueror but also a builder who had the vision to create a city that would rival all the great cities of the world. In this way, exile was not like being sent into slavery but like being placed in New York City or London or São Paulo, with great opportunity and material wealth. Nebuchadnezzar created one of the ancient wonders of the world with the Hanging Gardens, and his vision was unquenchable. Streets, districts, great walls, and temples have all been discovered through archaeological digs. His empire was an expansive display of power, economic resources, technological advancements of the day, and military might. By every account, Babylon was the superpower of the day.

The story of Babylon in the Bible is a story of empire and exile. To understand the story of Israel, we must understand the story of empire, or what we might call a superpower nation. Throughout biblical history, exile and empire lived together in a cause-and-effect relationship. People who experienced literal exile were usually forced into exile by an empire that had come against them.

The place Babylon holds within Scripture should give us pause when evaluating a nation's status of superpower. Scripture teaches that we should not equate being a superpower with God's blessing. If we associate God's blessing with national power, then we would certainly say that Israel did *not* have God's blessing. Rather, Egypt, Assyria, Babylon, Persia, and Rome were the bearers of God's blessing. But superior military might and economic power were not evidence of the blessing of the God of Scripture.

God used these nations for his divine purposes. In the case of the Israelites, he used Babylon to bring judgment on them. Prior to this judgment, one could say that the nation of Israel was a superpower. However, God intended that Israel be a different type of superpower. Through Israel and the Abrahamic blessing, all the nations of the world would be blessed. The blessing was not military and economic might. David's kingdom was to be a kingdom of God, not an empire of man. We see this in the warnings of Deuteronomy:

> When you enter the land the LORD your God is giving you and have taken possession of it and settled in it, and you say, "Let us set a king over us like all the nations around us," be sure to appoint over you a king the LORD your God chooses. He must be from among your fellow Israelites. Do not place a foreigner over you, one who is not an Israelite. The king, moreover, must not acquire great numbers of horses for himself or make the people return to Egypt to get more of them, for the LORD has told you, "You are not to go back that way again." He must not take many wives, or his heart will be led astray. He must not accumulate large amounts of silver and gold. When he takes the throne of his kingdom, he is to write for himself on a scroll a copy of this law, taken from that of the Levitical priests. It is to be with him, and he is to read it all the days of his life so that he may learn to revere the LORD his God and follow carefully all the words of this law and these decrees and not consider himself better than his fellow Israelites and turn from the law to the right or to the left. Then he and his descendants will reign a long time over his kingdom in Israel. (17:14–20)

The Davidic kingdom was meant to operate under a different set of rules than the other empires of the world. God was clear what kind of king Israel's king was supposed to be. Their king would not trust in his own power, his own wealth, his own pleasure but instead would worship and know the Lord. Israel would have a king who was a prince of the true King, Yahweh. In fact, God required a king not to think of himself as any better than the average Jew. Class distinctions within society had been the way of life in every culture. Royal blood meant something, but not for God's people. The king wasn't to see himself as any better than anyone else, because all of God's people have royal blood. Of course, the only king who perfectly executed this type of humble obedience was our King, Jesus, who gave us his royal blood as a seal that we belong to the Father as beloved sons and daughters.

God's Word also made it clear what would happen if the king and the people dishonored God and his instructions. If they defied God's vision of a kingdom in which the least and the last had dignity and opportunity, then God would bring punishment upon the king and his kingdom.

> The LORD will drive you and the king you set over you to a nation unknown to you or your ancestors. There you will worship other gods, gods of wood and stone. You will become a thing of horror, a byword and an object of ridicule among all the peoples where the LORD will drive you. (Deut. 28:36–37)

As the decades passed, king after king imitated the outward practices of the neighboring kingdoms and cultures, rejecting the vision God had for his king and his people. Judgment finally came, and God's people were carried off into captivity.

Enter Babylon

The Jews from the southern kingdom were taken captive in three separate deportations. Arriving in Babylon, they experienced lower-middle-class freedoms among the class of people known as the Mushkenu. Contrary to what most of us might think, they were not a part of the slave class known as the Wardu, as they were in Egypt. Many Jews started businesses, became prosperous, and contributed to the flourishing of Babylon.

Why did Nebuchadnezzar take these Jews captive and not place them into slavery? What was the upside of letting them lead lives in which they could prosper and make a decent life for themselves and their families? The primary objective for Nebuchadnezzar was to rid the exiles of their faith in the God of Abraham, Isaac, and Jacob and cause them to pledge their faithfulness to the gods of the new land. In short, Nebuchadnezzar wanted to assimilate the Jewish people, not persecute them, believing that they would exchange their faith in Yahweh for the pleasures of Babylon. The king hoped to subvert their worship of Yahweh through the conditions of security, comfort, wealth, and prosperity.

We can in some ways resonate with Nebuchadnezzar's tactics. The culture in which we live has created a similar type of captivity for God's people. In America, the church lives with relative religious freedom, and many followers of Jesus have been lulled to sleep. The cultural norms surrounding sex, money, and power have been practically adopted wholesale by many believers in their day-to-day lives. The power structures of many churches resemble the power structures of American businesses rather than the leadership teachings of the New Testament. In many ways, what Nebuchadnezzar sought to accomplish with the Jews in Babylon, our culture is accomplishing with Jesus's followers in North America today.

Entering Babylon, the people of God would have felt like my great-grandparents did as the world was changing around them. Only the experience of the Jews would have surpassed that of my ancestors. Everything about this new culture was different, and Nebuchadnezzar hoped that Babylon would soon become home to them and that their past would be replaced by the promises of Babylon.

The captivity that truly captured some of the Jews in exile was material captivity. When allowed to return to Israel, some opted to stay in Babylon, with its prosperity and material comfort, rather than return to Israel to try to rebuild a life and community. For these people, the glory of Babylon was of greater value than the glory of their God.

The captivity of materialism in Babylon is similar to the materialism that holds American Christians captive. Many Christians find their comfort, meaning, and security in the material offerings of a consumer culture. It is difficult not to be shaped by such a force. But the story of exile warns us that the power of wealth can turn the heart away from God. We will address this later through the practice of generosity. For now, we must see the importance of heeding the warning from Israel's story and seeing the parallel threat to our faith today.

Despite the comfort and freedoms of Israel's new surroundings, their loss was still a great source of pain, echoed in songs of lament as seen in Psalm 137:

By the rivers of Babylon we sat and wept
    when we remembered Zion.
There on the poplars
    we hung our harps,
for there our captors asked us for songs,
    our tormentors demanded songs of joy;
      they said, "Sing us one of the songs of Zion!"
How can we sing the songs of the LORD
    while in a foreign land? (vv. 1–4)

We can hear in the songs they sang that the Jews who worshiped Yahweh felt homesick walking the streets of Babylon. We may have difficulty wrapping our modern minds around all they had lost. The temple was gone, and their way of worship had been removed. The entire sacrificial system was no longer a part of their communal life together. The ways in which they worshiped God, received forgiveness of sins, and rehearsed their story of faith as God's people were in ruins. They were in a foreign land with foreign gods who seemed to have conquered their God and carried off his temple treasures, leaving the building in shambles.

It was also clear to them that they were not going home anytime soon. The prophet Jeremiah told them:

This is what the LORD Almighty, the God of Israel, says to all those I carried into exile from Jerusalem to Babylon: "Build houses and settle down; plant gardens and eat what they produce. Marry and have sons and daughters; find wives for your sons and give your daughters in marriage, so that they too may have sons and daughters. Increase in number there; do not decrease. Also, seek the peace and prosperity of the city to which I have carried you into exile.

Pray to the Lord for it, because if it prospers, you too will prosper." (29:4–7)

God commanded them not to listen to the so-called prophets who would tell them otherwise. But the situation was not without hope. Even though they were not returning anytime soon, God still had a plan for them:

"For I know the plans I have for you," declares the Lord, "plans to prosper you and not to harm you, plans to give you hope and a future. Then you will call on me and come and pray to me, and I will listen to you. You will seek me and find me when you seek me with all your heart. I will be found by you," declares the Lord, "and will bring you back from captivity." (Jer. 29:11–14)

They were lost but not forgotten, and so they didn't bury their heads in the sand or defect to the gods of Babylon. Some of the Jews turned to the Scriptures. In them, they discovered their identity as aliens and strangers in Babylon, and they continued to be the people of God. They developed new places of worship and new practices that formed their worshiping life as a community. Through the prophets' guidance, their time in Babylon would bring them into a more personal faith.

The temple they had lost, that sacred place of worship where they had met with God and made their sacrifices, was replaced with the synagogue. The large gatherings for communal worship and sacrifices for redemption were replaced with smaller gatherings in which they studied the Scriptures.

The people had freedom in Babylon to self-govern, not unlike our religious freedom, and priest and prophet were both recognized by the Jewish people and allowed to function by the Babylonian government. This tells us that they were not slaves in Babylon but had religious freedoms. Israel had to adjust what worship looked like without the temple, which led to the role of scribe arising out of a desire to study God's Word. Because most Jews spoke Aramaic, and the Scriptures were written in Hebrew, they needed both translators and interpreters, which became the work of the scribes. By the time of Jesus, the scribal interpretation had risen to being equal to the authority of the Scriptures themselves, and the teachers of the law were in hostile opposition to Jesus. Yet the scribal movement was healthy in its origins and only later became corrupted as people misused those teachings to gain control and create exclusion.

Faithfulness in Exile

When we think about how a person in urban America can offer their worship to Jesus or how a college student can admit they are a follower of Jesus, we are asking questions about faithfulness in a culture in which we are misunderstood and marginalized and misrepresented by other Christian voices. We are talking about how to be faithful in exile.

When we ask how a CEO of a large firm can lead his company as a Christian in today's climate of greed, financial shortcuts, and corporate takeovers, we are talking about how to be faithful in exile. When we consider an artist or an educator or so many more living out their faith often under the radar so as not to attract attention from the growing hostility that surrounds them, we are talking about living our faith in exile.

By looking at the situation of the Jews in Babylon, we can see that the times in which we find ourselves are nothing new for the people of God. The Babylonian exile offers a wealth of insight into what it means to be the people of God in a land in which we are growing continually marginalized. Through the key figures of the exile story, like the prophet Daniel, we can discover ways in which the people of God stood firm in their identity and lived out a faithful presence and a prophetic witness in their place and time.

As we look at the story of the Babylonian exile, we can see how God preserved his people during their time in Babylon. Despite the crisis moment for God's people, he led them to find a way to faithfulness in a dangerous and unfamiliar world.

By looking back into our history as followers of Jesus, we can find a way to look forward. We can discover a new way of being faithful and imagine fresh ways to practice our love and worship for the Father, Son, and Spirit.

Exile can be a place of deep spiritual transformation and kingdom advancement if we are willing to step into it with courage and faith. The good old days are behind us, and in front of us is a journey with many unknowns, but Jeremiah's promise to the exiles of his day is just as true for our exile moment: "'For I know the plans I have for you,' declares the LORD, 'plans to prosper you and not to harm you, plans to give you hope and a future'" (29:11).

FOUR

Baptize It, Burn It, or Bless It?

For the first three hundred years of the church's life, followers of Jesus lived in the type of exile that Peter described in his first letter. He wrote to followers of Jesus who had been scattered throughout Asia Minor. He identified them in two ways: God's elect (the chosen people of God) and exiles scattered abroad.

Life for these believers was one of suspicion and persecution. Their newfound faith had nowhere within mainstream culture to rest its head, and their way of life was viewed as peculiar. Despite their marginalized position within the broader society, though, Peter encouraged them to remember that God had chosen them, he was theirs and they were his, and despite their experience of suffering, they could trust and obey their God.

Given the circumstances these new believers faced, they could have easily fallen into despair and questioned God's plan. During the years that followed, things would only get worse. The apostles were martyred for their allegiance to Christ, and the church continued to be frowned upon at best and violently attacked at worst.

All that changed in the early days of the fourth century after Christ. In 312 AD, the Roman emperor Constantine was baptized and pronounced Christianity the religion of the Roman Empire. Over time, being baptized into the Christian faith became synonymous with citizenship in Rome. If you were a Christian living in the days of Constantine, you probably viewed his conversion and pronouncement as something God had orchestrated to further the gospel and establish his kingdom.

Persecution was over, and the faith that was once marginalized was now celebrated in the public square and the halls of government. The outcome seemed to be the total evangelization of the Roman Empire. The marginal place of the church in the broader culture was replaced with Christendom, uniting the church and the empire into one.

Christendom Defined

The term *Christendom* refers to that period of Christian history following Constantine's pronouncement in which the Christian religion was an integral and fundamental part of the social order. To be a full member of society, one also had to be a member of the church. The relationship of the state to the church changed from one of hostility or grudging acceptance to one of privilege and even affirmation. The strategy of Christendom became the conversion of the entire society to Christian faith and values, not just to the church within it.

Thus, in practice as well as in thought, much more attention had to be given to the relationship between the church and the state and the respective roles of the church and the state as different aspects of the one Christian social order.[1]

What was once a church in exile had now become a new social order that would continue in the West for the next fifteen hundred or so years. The people believed they were now a Christian society and the nations were Christian nations. Ironically, during this period, the empire did more to convert the church than the church did to convert the empire. A Christian nation is not the same thing as the church of God, even if their languages, values, and even practices to some extent look and sound the same.

Christianity as the state religion brought with it many implications. Because the Roman Empire was now "Christian," missions were no longer at the center of the church's life locally. Instead, missions became connected to military conquest of the non-Roman world. The military agenda of the Roman Empire could now be justified as doing the work of God, because to be taken under Roman rule was to be taken under the reign of Christ.

The marriage of church and state confused the church's identity as the people of God. As the culture at large adopted certain values of the Christian faith, the line between what it meant to be a follower of Jesus and what it meant to be a Roman citizen grew increasingly fuzzy.

Jesus gave strong warnings against this form of faith shaped by an empire because it was more about outward observance than an internal transformation of the heart. The dangers of putting one's faith in the empire, falling into the sin of ethnic pride, and finding security in the power and wealth of the empire were all alive and at work in weakening the church's allegiance to Jesus Christ.

These were the same sins for which Israel was judged by God, and they were the reason that the Israelites were taken into captivity. Ethnic pride caused Israel not to bless the "other" but to judge them harshly and to see them as less than. The people's security was not in the strength of Yahweh but in their economic and military power. The people's hearts turned away from their true faith in God and only through time and the judgment of God would it be recovered in Babylon.

American Civil Religion

A similar version of Christendom, in the form of a civil religion that assumed a general Judeo-Christian ethic, lived among us in America until the last several decades. The underlying belief was that God chose America to be a new type of Promised Land, freeing people from the class society of the British Empire and the religious conditions that took away their freedom to worship in a way their consciences allowed.

This democratic experiment led to the creation of the world's largest superpower, and religious freedom is one aspect that most of us happily enjoy. But we must be fair in our assessment, admitting that certain freedoms and privileges were not intended for all people. Our nation's history of war against native peoples and the endorsement of slavery are just two examples of how civil religion fell abundantly short of Christ and biblical Christianity.

The continued fallout of racism in our society and in our hearts lives on as a testimony to the perils of mixing Christian faith and civil religion. The result is a confusing picture of what Christianity is as it is reflected back to us by the media or in the public square.

The story of exile warns us, as it did the early church, of the dangers of putting our hope in the empire. For Christians who have trusted in national pride, ethnic pride, and economic and military security instead of trusting in Jesus, Israel's story warns that this misplaced trust leads to judgment.

National Pride

Faith in the American way of life, or national pride, found its way into the Christian faith for many Christians. Most churches placed the American flag in their sanctuaries below the cross, despite the law that states that the United States flag cannot be flown underneath any symbol of allegiance.[2] Putting the flag—a symbol for our allegiance to our country—in our churches, while perhaps well intended, spoke volumes regarding our national commitments and the assumption that they were closely aligned with the church's values and beliefs. If we imagined a German flag or a Russian flag in the same place within a sanctuary, we could see the problem more clearly. We would protest, arguing that the ideals and values of these other countries do not align with the teachings of Christ and his church. It is easy to see the discrepancies in other countries, but we have trouble seeing the same disconnects in our own culture.

Ethnic Pride

Ethnic pride is also evident in American society and in the American church. The concept of white privilege is not a twenty-first-century construct but resides deeply within our history as Americans. Insecurity felt by white Americans almost always comes in some form through the presence of people who do not share their ethnicity. We are still trying to explain who is included in "We the people" and which people were being referred to when the founders wrote that "all men are created equal." The effects of ethnic pride are seen throughout contemporary American culture, and this is evident in our churches, which continue to be one of the most segregated places in society. From Ferguson to Facebook, we are witnessing in real time that black lives may not matter in the same way that white lives matter. From historical race conflicts to the building of a wall along the Mexican border, the threat is always "the other." Those who are not like the majority are seen as inferior or a threat, and they are treated as such.

Economic and Military Security

The final feature of Israel's sin was putting their trust in military power and wealth. This stands to warn Christians in America that placing our hope in the economy and the military above our hope in Christ leads us to the same unfaithfulness of which Israel was guilty. Yet these are significant foundations upon which American life is built. To threaten these two pillars of security is to threaten the American way of life.

Every nation must find a way to protect its interests and secure itself against perceived threats to its national security. But the Bible doesn't easily support military conquests and aggressive economic practices. As a result, doctrines such as "just war" and "manifest destiny" began to emerge. But history teaches us that empires that try to justify their practices biblically create ethical quandaries that are not easily defended with Scripture.

Security for the people of God is in God alone, be it personal security or national security. This does not mean we should not support the military or economic strategy, but these things cannot be our ultimate hope as the people of God. When our hope becomes misplaced in these things, we begin to see other countries as a threat rather than a neighbor.

Honestly evaluating where our ultimate security lies can help us see if and where our hearts have strayed from God. We cannot be faithful to God if we find our ultimate security in our national military and economic power rather than in the abiding presence of Christt.

These pillars of national pride, ethnic pride, and economic and military security have been alive and well in American society, and these same sins were in large part the reason for Israel's judgment. Living just under the surface of our attitudes and actions, these false securities ultimately lead us into a misplaced trust and hope.

A New Babylon

We now find ourselves in a time when Christendom in the form of civil religion has come to an end. The assumption that to be an American is to hold Christian values is long past. Many factors contributed to this shift in American society. One summary of these factors is found in the *New Dictionary of Theology*:

It has taken the combination of the Enlightenment, secularization, political revolution and reform, and the development of a pluralistic social order finally to destroy the reality of Christendom. Only the memories remain, in aspects of our culture and in folk religion.[3]

It is beyond the scope of this book to analyze all the factors that led us to this moment, but what is clear is that we live in a new Babylon, an empire that does not at its core celebrate or at times even tolerate the beliefs, values, and practices of the Christian faith. We may hear a certain level of lip service given to these values and beliefs, but at the core, they are not a driving force for the culture at large.

America is now a post-Christian society, and amid the myriad changes that have accompanied this shift, the church must answer the questions, What does it mean to be the people of God now? And what does faithfulness look like in the empire in which we live? Failures and successes, written in history and the Bible, give us opportunity to reimagine what faithfulness can look like for us in North America and other Western contexts today. As the people of God in exile, should we try to turn Babylon into a Christian nation? Should we burn it down and build something better? How do we discover anew how to be the people of God in this time and this place?

Baptize Babylon

One temptation is to baptize all that is Babylon and call it good, as if all its cultural wares are for our pleasure and benefit. This is always a great temptation for God's people whenever they find themselves in a moment like ours. In this way, the sexual values of the culture are adopted by the church, and literal interpretations of Scripture are replaced by a more liberal rendering of Jesus's teaching. Issues on the table for discussion include Jesus being the only way to the Father, saving yourself sexually for marriage, and lots of other dos and don'ts, which many feel should be done away with. If the culture says something is good, then the church falls in step to keep up with the times and preserve a place within the broader cultural narrative.

Baptizing Babylon can also look like consumerism—that one "ism" that people living in American culture find nearly impossible to escape. It is easy for someone to think of themselves as a good Bible-believing follower of Jesus, all the while spending more money than they make to buy the things that make them feel secure and fulfilled. Their personal theology may be conservative, but what they believe about spending money and purchasing products never gets touched by their theology.

We can also baptize Babylon through a constant consumption of entertainment and technology. A church that was once overly strict about going to movies as a form of cultural resistance is now led by pastors who don't think twice about binge-watching Netflix for countless hours a week. We find ways to promote more glamorous versions of our lives on social media that have little resemblance to our actual lives, and yet we feel a sensation of hope and meaning when our posts are liked or retweeted. Without bowing a knee to a wooden statue of a false god, we offer our identity to the technologies of our day and allow our interactions to shape and form our own self-understanding.

There is a lot more going on in Babylon than what is written in our doctrinal statements. We are ignorant to think that those who hold to a more conservative theology are not at risk of being assimilated by cultural forces at work all around us. Our understanding of power, money, pleasure, and success are all shaped by the word on the streets of Babylon. These forces have always been at work threatening the church's faithfulness to Jesus. This is not new to God's people. The subtle forces are usually the most dangerous to our souls. When we conform to cultural forces on the right or the left, we begin to be assimilated by the culture, and it is impossible to be faithful to Jesus and assimilated to culture simultaneously. If we are going to be faithful in exile, Jesus must be our ultimate source of truth and security.

The way forward will require us to move beyond doctrinal divides of conservative and liberal. We will need to find a set of practices, born from faith, that can make us distinct in our identity and our way of living in this new moment in which we find ourselves.

Burn Down Babylon

It is human nature to place blame. Followers of Jesus need to be careful here, because putting the blame on others has been the way of the human heart since the fall of Adam. The church has taken this approach for many years and effected little change in the broader culture.

It is easy to stand inside our self-made cathedrals and point our fingers at the outside world and blame "those people" for their moral failings. It is also easy to believe that we can end our exile by "fixing" the outside world—in effect, burning down Babylon—by legislating culture to fit the values of the church. This has been especially true regarding the biblical definition of marriage.

When we first started the church I pastor, I received a letter announcing that if my church did not support legislation that defined marriage as the joining of one man and one woman, there would be consequences. The most adamant threat was that our failure to comply would cost us donations once they let it be widely known. The people who drafted the letter told us that Western civilization was at risk, and they assumed we were not on the side of truth.

I was struck that biblical marriage as defined in Scripture was being equated with civil marriage in American culture. This seemed ironic to me, in that the rate of divorce within church and culture are both around 50 percent. It is clear that just because a marriage is between one man and one woman does not mean it is a God-honoring, Christ-exalting union that points to the mystery of our union with Christ. Scripture is clear that God hates divorce. Divorce is a painful event, and when it happens, everyone suffers. God's teachings about it are not harsh and unfeeling; they are preserving words with the hopes of protecting people from deep pain.

So it struck me as odd that little was being done to curb the divorce rate within the church. Marital fidelity is sorely lacking among the faithful, and no one would consider legislation to remove no-fault divorce from the laws of the land.

The point being that blaming the people outside the church for the marginalization of the church's values in the culture is a pointless exercise. It simply comes off as a futile attempt to avoid the inevitable marginalization of believers.

Richard Mouw illustrates how, in our attempts to legislate Christian values, we subtly quit trusting in Jesus and begin to trust political powers that we hope will secure our values:

> The criticisms of the Constantinian arrangement are legitimate. When the church allies itself too closely with political power it loses the freedom to be the kind of church that God wants it to be. The late Lesslie Newbigin, who served for many years during the twentieth century as a missionary in India, made this case very effectively. When Newbigin returned to the British Isles after his retirement, he was shocked by the major cultural changes that had taken place there as well as on the European continent and in North America. When he began his career, he saw himself as being sent out from a Christian culture—where Christianity was "the established religion"—to a mission field. But now he realized that his own homeland had become a mission field. Christians in the West, Newbigin observed, could no longer take a dominant Christian influence for granted. We are now, he said, "post-Christendom." But that is not a thing to be regretted, he quickly added; the church should always see itself as "missional." The Christendom arrangement lured the church into a sense of "owning" the culture that kept it from full faithfulness to the gospel.[4]

Bless and Resist Babylon

If the answer to what it means to be the people of God now is not to baptize Babylon and it is not to burn Babylon to the ground in hopes that we can reconstruct a new and better Christendom, then what alternatives do we have at our disposal?

What we will discover is that Israel in exile gives us great insight into living in this new world. As we are about to see, the way in which the people of God navigated their faithfulness to God in exile was not to burn Babylon or to baptize Babylon but to find distinct ways in which to bless and resist Babylon. In the process, they discovered ways to be faithful in the given moment in which they found themselves. They teach us how we might find a way forward for ourselves as we follow an ancient path into this volatile new world.

There are several lessons to be learned from those who were faithful to God in exile. By looking into how they navigated these tricky waters, we discover that in exile we must learn to live faithfully to God without the power and privilege of holding a majority position in society or in the world. Exile reveals to us that our hope is in another kingdom, with the currency of love, where we are all one in Christ and the weapons of our warfare are prayer and sacrifice in the name of Jesus.

The faithful in Babylon also show us that in exile we must learn to be faithful in our presence and prophetic in our witness, while participating in the world through practices that create an alternative narrative of what it means to be the people of God in public spaces and in personal callings.

The prophets of that time proclaimed loud and clear that history is not under the control of other gods, nor can its mysteries be discovered by human manipulation. History is under the control of the God who is utterly free to direct it and to reveal it as he pleases (Rev. 5:9). According to his sovereign pleasure, he will intervene among the kingdoms of this world and establish a universal kingdom that will endure forever.

The God of Israel in exile is the God of the church in twenty-first-century America. And this is the God who is still free to direct the course of history and reveal himself to his people and to the world as he pleases.

FIVE

Discerning Faithfulness in Exile

The challenge I feel every day pastoring in Portland, Oregon, is discerning what faithfulness to Jesus looks like now. Portland is a city that is proud of being progressive. Like those in many urban centers, people in Portland pride themselves on their liberal politics, biking through inches of rain to save the environment, and being spiritually open-minded but never religious, an open-mindedness that Ravi Zacharias would liken to the sewer rejecting nothing and accepting everything,[1] everything but Christianity for the most part. Zacharias shows the implicit problem with being open to everything. Any coherent view of reality will automatically reject certain things.

Culture Makes Disciples

Portland is great at making disciples. All cultures that have defining characteristics are discipling cultures. The power of the cultural values leads people to conform to those values, and that can be seen in how they think, act, and believe. The TV show *Portlandia*, a spoof of Portlanders, is only somewhat of an exaggeration. A good portion of people in Portland don't really get the joke, because in Portland the parody is the reality—at least in some places.

Portland is, in a way, my exile. It is my home, but it is not my home at the same time. Home for me is California, where the sun comes out and people don't measure the yearly rainfall using fifty-gallon barrels. At nineteen, I left that sunny state, and I never went back. Since then, for all but a short stint in a small town to the east, Portland has been my home.

With its naked bike rides boasting over ten thousand participants yearly and people who are more pro-dog than pro-life, this is the place where God put me, and this is the place where thousands of Jesus followers are finding a way toward faithfulness even as a dominant culture remains unwelcoming of such an endeavor.

While not every city will go the way of Portland, the general ethos of my city is becoming the norm in urban centers. The famous bumper sticker "Keep Portland Weird" is losing its punch as weird becomes the new normal in most cities.

Finding Our Way to Faithfulness

Finding our way to faithfulness presents a challenge that we as the church in our city have not exactly figured out. But we have learned a lot in striving toward Christ and his calling to be the people of God who bear witness to Jesus in his life, death, resurrection, and present reign. That's a mouthful, and the complexities of doing that are inherent in the sentence itself. The task is no small thing.

But this is the task that Jesus gave the church, and it is a discipling task. The question we are wrestling with in our cultural moment, How are we to be the people of God now? is one that Jesus's followers in more progressively liberal cities have been wrestling with for a long time, and one God's people have been working out since their inception in Abraham's blessing. How did they do it? What can we learn from how they navigated their moment?

Contextualizing the Gospel

Lesslie Newbigin was a British theologian and missiologist who served most of his career as a missionary in India. Newbigin thought deeply about the interplay between the gospel, the church, and culture. When he returned to the United Kingdom, he was shocked by the ways in which the church of the West had embraced modernity, with its scientific rationalism, without questioning if modernity itself was a biblical worldview.

Newbigin made it his mission to recover the missionary identity of the church in the West, and his writings have influenced countless missionaries, theologians, and pastors over the last several decades.

One of Newbigin's most profound contributions was rescuing the gospel from culture. Newbigin argued that the gospel is essentially a-cultural, meaning it does not exist with a culture tied to it but instead enters a given place and contextualizes itself to that culture. It is a living proclamation that when preached and lived out within a culture will critique and transform the people of that place. A new entity is then born and established—the church.

Ours is a time when the gospel is not new, and the church in America dates back to when the Pilgrims settled on our soil. This history is no small matter when trying to understand the current missionary task of the church. A familiarity with Christianity and the presence of church buildings in every community lead to the assumption that the church and its message have been here and done that. The problem with this assumption is that while the roots of the church have grown deep in the American soil, that soil has shifted, and the roots have lost their footing. As a result, we need a new way of being the people of God in this moment. The way, however, is as old as the message we offer. It is the way of mission. The church is always and everywhere tasked to bring the message of Jesus in fresh ways to the culture in which it finds itself. We must continue to try to understand our new place and understand what makes the message of Christ good news to those who are building their lives here.

This means the church must learn to navigate its relationship to the culture it finds itself in at this moment. There is no command for the church to recover yesterday or the day before. The gospel is public truth for this moment and every moment to come, and as a result, we must be a public people who embody this message in public spaces. We are in an interdependent relationship with the culture in which we live.

I can hear the protest going on in some of your minds. We are not a part of the culture. We have been saved out of the culture. There is no interdependence between the church and the culture.

Let me ask you this: Where did you buy your groceries this week? What did you use to purchase them? How did you get to the grocery store? How did you get the money for the groceries? Where did you bring the groceries once you bought them?

Everything we do happens within the culture in which we live. From the way we dress to the jobs we go to, everything in our lives takes place within a given space on the map. This is also the place we practice our faith in Christ. Any other understanding is an illusion. If you work and take a paycheck, you shop and buy the culture's wares, how can you honestly believe you don't have an interdependent relationship with the culture?

We all live within culture, and therefore we must pay attention to how we as the community of God's people understand our place within culture. We also need a fresh perspective of how to take the gospel into this place we call home.

The problems Newbigin saw upon his return were many. In his estimation, the church was losing or had lost the true sense of what it means to be the people of God and in doing so was at risk of replacing the gospel with its own culturally shaped understandings of God, the Scriptures, the church, and faith. He called this a new form of gnosticism.

In his attempt to define the interplay between the gospel, the church, and culture, Newbigin and those who followed him, such as the Church Between Gospel and Culture Network, created what has become known as the Newbigin Triangle (see the figure on the next page). As we examine it, we can see how the church is meant to interact with the gospel and culture in a way that allows it to remain faithful to the gospel and redemptive in its relationship to the place in which it lives.

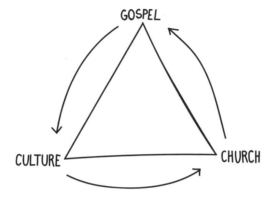

If we follow the arrows, they help us understand how the gospel travels. As the gospel is preached and displayed in a given culture, people contextualize it for that culture. In doing this, Jesus's life, death, resurrection, and ascension are communicated in word and deed through the power of the Holy Spirit.

Contextualization looks different in each culture in which the gospel is announced, or at least it should. We see this in the book of Acts. After Jesus's ascension, Peter, full of the Holy Spirit, stood up and preached his first message to a mostly Jewish audience. Using the Psalms and the Prophets, Peter communicated the gospel in the language and the cultural context of the Jewish people. While they listened and the Spirit worked on their hearts, they heard that Jesus was the fulfillment of the Davidic promise and that the prophets of old foretold his coming (Acts 2).

Fast-forward to Acts 17, and we find Paul in Athens on Mars Hill. The Athenians were a very different crowd, both in their understanding of themselves and in their faith and concepts of God. Paul didn't take them back to the Old

Testament and lead them down a path through the Prophets. Instead, he found an idol to an unknown God. The city was full of idols, and Paul took note of that. He told them that he could see they were very religious/spiritual people. He quoted Cretan poetry to them, which they were familiar with. Then he told them who the unknown God was: the risen Lord and Savior, Jesus Christ.

Think about the radical difference between Peter's preaching and Paul's. Paul used an idol to lead people to Jesus. If Peter had done that, the crowd would have rioted. The Jewish people were well versed in the sin of idolatry and idol worship. To make a leap from an idol to the Messiah would have seemed to them like heresy.

But this was not the case for Paul. Paul was free to contextualize the gospel to this very different crowd. He discerned who they were, what they valued, and how best to tell them about Jesus. He was a rabbi turned disciple who had been raised on the Jewish Scriptures. He knew what he was doing, and at the same time, he had the freedom in the Spirit to communicate to the people in their cultural moment the timeless message of Christ that is never owned by any one culture.

Using Windows of Redemption and Opposition

Every culture on earth has what I call windows of redemption and windows of opposition. Every culture values things that are good, true, and beautiful, and through these windows of redemption, we can find ways to talk about Jesus. For Peter, the window was the Jewish crowd's religious history and familiarity with the poets and the prophets of the Old Testament. For Paul, it was the religious climate of

Athens. Even though the religious climate had resulted in idol worship, Paul could tap into the people's hunger for transcendence to tell them about the true God.

In Portland, a redemptive window may be the arts, where people place a deep value on creativity. By engaging the arts as the people of God, we can join a conversation on creativity but motivated by our faith and theology. We create not simply for self-expression but because we were created by a God who is endlessly creative.

Another window may be environmental advocacy. People in Portland care about the environment, and as followers of Jesus, we believe that we have been commissioned by God to steward his creation. This value that we hold in common for very different reasons may be a way for us to begin a conversation about God.

Portland also has many vulnerable people, from victims of sex trafficking to foster children to homeless families and individuals living on our streets. When we follow Jesus's command to care for the widows and the orphans and the least of these, we often work shoulder to shoulder with civic leaders and other individuals who have an equal concern for these populations in our city. As a result, we find ourselves in relationships with people who, though they have different motives, care about the things God cares about. As the church enters these spaces, we have a powerful ministry of presence and can use the open doors of proclamation given to us.

Every culture values something that God calls good or true or beautiful, and those are the places where that culture is open to the redemptive possibilities that Jesus brings. No culture lacks these windows of redemption. We all have been created in the image of God, and because of that image-bearing reality, we are wired on the inside for the good and true and beautiful because those things reflect the nature and character of God. They get twisted, marred, and perverted, but they are there underneath the surface if we just take the time to look. Through these windows of redemption, we can engage the culture in its own space and through its own language and values. We can establish relationships while we follow the Holy Spirit into his work of making Jesus known. We are participants and mouthpieces seeking to live lives congruent to what we say we believe.

There are also windows of opposition in every culture. These are the values, beliefs, and practices that are at odds with Jesus and the gospel. Seeing them requires that we discern good and evil. Then we must thoughtfully engage our neighbors concerning issues that we disagree on. Both Peter and Paul, though differing in their presentation of the gospel, called for people to repent. That word means "to turn." The turn required in every culture is from self to Jesus as King over all things.

As we try to discern what the windows of opposition are, we also need to identify what they are not. We must be careful to separate what is opposed to Jesus and the gospel and what is simply opposed to our church culture or rules that exist within the larger culture. An example of this can be seen in the Western missionary movement. When the church in the West sent missionaries into the world a hundred or so years ago, they often brought their cultural values with them, and too often they imposed those values on native cultures. Those values included manifest destiny, which claimed that God wanted to give Westerners the land of the Native Americans. It also involved teaching African children to sing hymns in Latin, dress in Western fashions of the day, and play the violin. Those were cultural impositions, not gospel contextualization.

If we look closer at these two examples, we can learn how things got muddled. In manifest destiny, the desire to conquer the new world was inextricably tied to God, who was believed to be granting white Americans the authority to take land and convert those whom they considered savages—the Native Americans. The call to proclaim the good news was mixed with the imperial call to conquer new lands, which perverted the first calling. By wedding God and country into one over-arching belief system or worldview, Christians opened the door to committing atrocities in the name of God for the sake of country. If they had seen the New World through the lens of biblical missionary mandates, it's possible that the connection between gospel proclamation and conquering land would have been broken and the native people's way of life preserved. The gospel could have fit into Native American culture, and Jesus could have been worshiped and proclaimed in the language, music, and customs of the native peoples, though some of those customs would have needed to be transformed to reflect faith in Christ. In short, the church could have grown in its diversity and understanding of God through the expression of faith practiced by native cultures in their own cultural traditions. The church would have seen a reflection of Jesus redeeming and transforming people as they were in their culture, not as another culture demanded them to be.

This doesn't mean that certain values and customs should not be critiqued and challenged. How does a person love their neighbor in a culture that teaches them it's okay to eat their neighbor? Cannibals need to be converted to neighborly love in their culture. And in a consumer culture, we have our own ways of cannibalizing our neighbors instead of loving them. The gospel has a strong critique of every culture because every culture in some way is a godless culture that requires Jesus's redemption and transformation.

Confronting windows of opposition within a culture can be very challenging. If we go to war against the people who believe certain things are not sin, we misrepresent Jesus's love and compassion to them. But if we just ignore those issues, we misrepresent Jesus's truth and authority to them. It is the tightrope we walk. How do we do both faithfully?

This is why being faithful to Jesus requires discernment, because Jesus loves people enough to die for them, and he is the hope of the world. We hold this truth carefully and seek to carry it faithfully, so that those who hear and see the gospel that we announce, see and hear it accurately represented as "Good News." So how do we do this well? First, we need to understand how the gospel interacts with the church and culture.

Church Culture Is Not the Gospel

For too long, we have held up the culture of the church, instead of the gospel of Jesus, as the plumb line for what is good or bad.

Once I led a group of rural students on a trip to the city for a concert. Along the way, we stopped at a movie, and in the evening, a group of us played cards. After the trip, one of the leaders confronted me, and I found out that he had been raised to believe that both going to the movies and playing cards were taboo for anyone who follows Jesus. I was not raised in the church. I had never even heard of those rules. The kids who were with us hadn't either. The card game could hardly have been referred to as gambling, and the movie was definitely not R rated. The clash that was occurring was over what a Christian can and cannot do.

The process we had to work through was a matter of discernment. What was it about Jesus and his gospel, or the whole of Scripture for that matter, that would make rules like that necessary? After a few meetings and several conversations, we identified that those rules that he felt were being broken were not Jesus's rules. They were a part of the church culture he had been raised in and had been given a type of divine authority by the leaders of his church. But they had no basis in the gospel.

If anyone from my family heard that Jesus loved them and never wanted them to play cards or go to the movies again, only part of that would sound like good news.

We have built walls of self-protection around us that are man-made, not God ordained. The mistake here is believing that sin comes from outside of us when Jesus told us that it comes from inside of us. We can't build fences tall enough to keep sin from showing up in our own hearts (see Mark 7:20). The example above is from church culture of the late 1950s and '60s. The types of rules have changed in terms of the actual dos and don'ts, but they are still values of the church's moralistic culture, not the gospel of Jesus.

Today the rules might be different. In some places, like Portland, the pendulum has swung. If you're a "liberated" Christian, then drinking a microbrewed IPA is a freedom second only to salvation! The idea that you would give that up to help a person who has struggled with alcoholism might feel like an infringement on your right to imbibe. The freedom to drink can become a sign we wave to show we aren't stuffy, old-school fundamentalists, assuming anyone who doesn't share that freedom is less free, less spiritual, just less than . . . us.

The sad reality is that most followers of Jesus don't know how to discern what is sin and what is life-giving because so much of their discipling has been focused on personal conduct and not spiritual discernment.

One man who came to Christ in his midtwenties described it this way: "After I met Jesus, most people I met were really worried about who I was sleeping with, but no one asked me about my money and how I spent it." He recognized that in the culture of the church, sexual sin is at the top of the list, but the sins of greed and overconsumption rarely get mentioned. Jesus wants our entire lives. This means he wants not only our sexual fidelity but also our generosity as we use our money for his kingdom instead of to serve ourselves.

To navigate the road of faithfulness, we need to be ruthless with ourselves and allow the whole of Jesus's teaching, not just what a certain church deems good or bad, to bring us to conviction and transformation. We need to hear the gospel in a fresh way for ourselves. The gospel is as much for the church as it is for the world. If we are going to be faithful in exile, then we will need ongoing conversion. That is what I want to talk about next.

SIX

The Ongoing Conversion of God's People

Two skills are critical for God's people in exile. The first is repentance and the second is discernment.

The First Skill Needed: Developing the Discipline of Repentance

Why repentance? To be a faithful presence and a prophetic witness, we must admit both that we don't know how to do that and perhaps that we don't even want to. A continuing theme for Israel and for the people of God is a return to the Lord, to seek his face with all our hearts and to be transformed by the power of his Spirit. The promise God gives to us is that we will find him when we seek him with all our hearts. In our hearts, we find both the presence of sin that gives life to sinful behaviors and the tendency toward selfishness that makes us incapable of loving others in the way we are called to. If we are to survive exile, we need a radical conversion of our hearts to change both what we love and how we live.

Heart Issues

The problem lies in our hearts, as Jesus told us it did (Mark 7:21). That problem can't be behaved away, and decades of moralism have led to statistical proof of that fact. The problem is not in the behaviors themselves but in the deeper issues of our hearts.

It is not just the sinful things in our hearts that cause the problem; it's also the absence of the right things—the absence of love for our neighbors, the absence of care for the poor, the absence of compassion for the prisoner and the brokenhearted. While not everyone is guilty, we as Christians are often collectively known for what we are against rather than for *whom* Jesus was for. His selfless love and compassion, which led to his sacrifice, were the fruit of a love that every one of us desperately desires and longs for.

The issue with moralism is this: as hard as we try to keep the bad stuff out, we can never manufacture the good stuff— the love, joy, peace, patience, kindness, and goodness that allow us to give ourselves away for the sake of another. The only way to true spiritual whole-life transformation is to get our hearts right.

So how do we get our hearts right?

Hearts Open before Jesus

When we started our church in Portland, we had a small band of young people. Their average age was probably twenty-two, and that was only due to a couple in their fifties who bumped the age up. Most of the people in the group of about twenty were first- or second-year college students. We spent about six months talking about being a church that existed for the world and not for ourselves. We loved to talk about this subject. We read about it and discussed it in small groups, and we were becoming experts on the philosophy and theology of mission.

The one thing that didn't happen during those six months was that we didn't do any of the things we read and talked about. We remained an insular group of people who enjoyed talking about God but did not live our lives for him as a living sacrifice, myself included.

I remember when I finally realized the problem. In America, we assume that our primary issue, when it comes to faith or any other topic, is that we need more information to understand how to do the thing we want to do. This is true from weight loss to worship. We assume we lack information and believe that if we only had the right information, then we would naturally do the thing we want to do. What we really lack is not information but the appropriate desires that move us toward the right things. The only person who can change the desires deep within us is Jesus. Our small congregation didn't have a how-to problem; we had a want-to problem, and only Jesus could change it.

I realized that I had to get myself and this little community to Jesus. We needed him to change our hearts, our minds, our affections, and our desires. Nothing in my bag of leadership tricks could change my own heart, let alone those of the people I was pastoring.

I will never forget the night I announced my big plan. We sat in a dimly lit room with flickering candles, and it felt as though we were about to hear a bunch of monks sing a Gregorian chant. I had very little confidence in my idea, but I didn't have any better ones at that point.

I announced that we were going to start meeting on Wednesday nights to repent. I know, not a very attractive description for my new event. "Hey, bring all your friends. We're going to repent together on Wednesday!" Doesn't really sound great, right?

I confessed my own lack of an authentic desire to be on mission and the realization that we liked to hang out together because we loved one another. We liked to talk about Jesus and mission and the city and the Bible and what the church should be, but if we were honest with ourselves, we didn't want to do any of it. We didn't want to change, we didn't want to love the people Jesus loves, and we didn't want to go to the places Jesus was sending us.

We needed to repent. *Repent* is a word that has become scandalous in modern-day American churches, but it is a word that needs to be resurrected. It is a word of hope, of change, of anticipation. It means to turn around because there's something better, something new, but the idea is counterintuitive because we have to go back to go forward. It's a word so full of hope and promise that it was the first word on John the Baptist's lips when he announced God's kingdom: "Repent, for the kingdom of heaven has come near" (Matt. 3:2).

Repentance is the way to get our hearts open and honest before God, the real God face-to-face with the real us. No more hiding behind religious speech and pious façades.

We needed to encounter the gospel for ourselves before we could offer it to others—not the reductionist, punch-your-ticket-and-get-into-heaven gospel but the robust, never-ending gospel for which initial faith is simply the doorway into continual, lifelong transformation.

In order to live faithfully in exile, in order to have the missionary attitude of faithfulness and prophetic witness, we need to be continually transformed by the gospel of Jesus. His teachings, his life, his love, and his Spirit need to shed light on our lack of love and compassion and our selfish aspirations. His Spirit convicts and we confess. His Spirit replaces our self-focus with his others-centered agenda.

This little band of Jesus followers had stumbled upon the beautiful secret of living faithfully as a spiritual community: the need to be continually converted by the Spirit of God to the heart of God and the mission of God.

This isn't theory either; this happened. The beautiful thing about this group was their willingness to be honest. But the thing I remember cringing over was that they were being really honest.

"Jesus, I don't like my neighbor, and I am too busy to get to know him."

"God, I am not convinced that you are even there."

"God, I don't want to love the people you love. Honestly, it's scary and I don't think I am up for it."

This went on and on for an hour and a half until I couldn't take it anymore. I closed the meeting with a sweet little prayer ditty I'd been taught in Bible college.

Driving home, I remember wondering what my next job would be, since I was sure I had just killed whatever church I had just started. It turns out I did kill it, but in a good way. What we thought church should be needed to be crucified and resurrected. Our plans of what we wanted the life of faith to be needed to be buried and raised to life by the Author and

Perfecter of our faith. We needed the Holy Spirit to change our hearts.

The Slow Arch of Repentance Leads to Change

We continued to meet, and I look back on those Wednesday nights with fond memory. Over time, something started to change. Authentic desire that can only come from the heart of Jesus started to show up in our lives. Heather, Missy, and Kindra found a rehab center for single moms and spent the next several years going weekly to care for those women. Joe started cooking on a Coleman stove on Saturdays at three o'clock. Over the years, hundreds of homeless people gathered for food, conversation, and the knowledge that someone cared. Three O'Clock People was born, and for the next fifteen years, people came to the east side of the city, rain or shine, to feed and be with the hundreds of people living on the streets.

These were signs of spiritual transformation. Hearts were being converted, and the actual life of Jesus was breaking through. Over a decade and a half later, we continue to see Jesus converting us through his gospel week in and week out. The results are inspiring.

Members of the church are caring for hundreds of foster children and families and advocating for the victims of sex trafficking. Artists are using their gifts to mentor and inspire young students. People are giving generously to build clean water projects in villages all over Africa. The things that God has birthed out of our little community astound me, and they are too numerous to list. Hundreds have been baptized and are experiencing new life that only Jesus can give. We are learning to be the people of God in exile and to bless the city in which we live. We have a long way to go, but mustard-seed miracles are sprouting up all over the city. Followers of Jesus are announcing another kingdom in some of the hardest-hit areas where people are forgotten. There may be no place in Babylon for the least and the last, but in the kingdom of God, there is always an extra seat at the table.

I share a few of these stories to show that what happened in our church is not the result of any program or moralistic agenda. This is the fruit of conversion. When we give our hearts to Jesus, he slowly and over time replaces our desires with his. Revolution occurs.

The church needs this type of conversion. There are no maps; we are walking through uncharted territory. We have something better though. The Lord of Daniel and Jeremiah is with us. The one who guided his people through Babylon, the ascended Christ who led Peter and the exiles he wrote to in his letters, will guide us through our exile too.

But we must be willing to repent. We must be willing to be honest with ourselves, to be broken over the state of our own hearts and the part we played in making the church the way it is.

So many people are blogging and tweeting at one another and placing blame on one another. What we don't hear is confession. Confession is the birthplace of repentance and, as such, the birthplace of conversion. The gospel does not call us to publicly defend our positions on social media and place blame on others. Jesus clearly calls us to a radical love that is greater than our differences, a love that allows us to look inside ourselves and to be honest about our own sin that has contributed to the lack of unity and love in the family of

God and the polarization in our communities at large. This love calls us to sacrifice for those we disagree with. Even our enemies are objects of love in Jesus's family.

We need less tweeting and more confessing. We need honest bloggers who care more about the God who reads their hearts than the fans who read their posts. We need pastors and leaders who will open the pages of Scripture and have the spiritual courage to take their place at the foot of the cross as sinners desperate for grace and mercy to flow on them and in them from the wounds of Christ. We need to be converted to the heart of Jesus. When that happens, mission will follow.

The Second Skill Needed: Developing the Discipline of Discernment

When we grow in familiarity with our own continual conversion, we will also grow in our ability to discover what faithfulness looks like in exile.

One of the characteristics of exile is that it is unfamiliar. The new world around us doesn't share our values. There are no categories for our truth claims. The culture is an uneasy place to express and live out our beliefs. Because this new place has its own powerful values, truths, and beliefs, we have difficulty knowing when to bless and love and when to resist and take a stand.

One of the gifts that the Spirit of God gives his people is the ability to discern. Discernment is the ability to know how to be faithful to Jesus in a particular situation. Discernment helps bring correction when we fall into separatist religion or syncretistic conformity. As we grow in our practice of confession and repentance, our conversion process will help us discern what faithfulness looks like in each situation.

Discernment like Daniel's

I think of Daniel when I think of discernment. Daniel was one of the nobles of Israel. He was young, smart, and good-looking. In exile, he found himself in an entirely new world. His customs, his religion, his people had all gone missing. He was taken along with other young men like himself and trained in Babylonian language, politics, governance, and customs of the people. The first thing the Babylonians did was change his name. Daniel, which means "God is my judge," was replaced with Belteshazzar, which means "Bel protect the king."

Comparing the names themselves, we can feel the tension in which Daniel was living. His calling to faithfulness with God as his judge put Daniel into tension with his new vocation in exile of serving and protecting the king. Daniel and his friends had difficult decisions to make, and in most cases, they didn't have time in the moment to consult their elders and gain wisdom from their spiritual leaders.

We see Daniel practicing discernment in the very first chapter of Daniel. The king decreed that the captives who were in training to serve him were to eat the royal food, but for some reason Daniel refused. Perhaps the food was sacrificed to idols; we aren't told. We only know that when it came to the food of the royal palace, Daniel resisted. He asked that he and his friends be given only vegetables, and the guard could decide for himself after ten days if they were lacking in strength. As Daniel 1:15 tells us, "At the end of the ten days they looked healthier and better nourished than any of the young men who ate the royal food."

God was with Daniel in Babylon. That is the sum of the book. God is the Lord of history, and even in exile he's at work behind the scenes.

The question that I have when I read this story is this: Why did Daniel throw down the gauntlet on the food? They changed his name from a faith-filled Hebrew name to a pagan name that reduced him to a role of protecting the king who had sacked his people. Why didn't he refuse the name and eat the meat?

The short answer is we don't know. All we know is that Daniel was a man who was faithful in exile. The Spirit of God helped Daniel discern what that faithfulness looked like for him in his time and place. Faithfulness for Daniel meant resisting the meat and letting the Babylonians call him by a pagan name. For his moment of exile, this was prophetic resistance. When it came to eating the royal food, he drew a line. In terms of his name, he didn't resist at all. He served the kings of Babylon his entire life under that name.

The Main Question

Discernment in exile may not make sense to those on the outside looking in. Being misunderstood is par for the course. Our main concern is not "What will people think of me?"; it is "What does my faithfulness to Jesus mean in this situation? How do I discern when to bless and when to resist right here and right now?"

Knowing the heart of Christ is critical for this task. When do our actions draw people to Christ and his beauty, and when do they reveal his truth and his holiness? When do we pass on the steak and let them call us names?

There isn't a prescriptive way to do this, because gospel discernment is the fruit of a relationship with Jesus through the Spirit. When we walk in the Spirit, we can discern how the love and goodness of Jesus become good news to the people we are sent to love. When we are in step with the Spirit, we are more likely to feel his conviction when we have slipped into self-protection or cultural assimilation instead of self-less love and holiness.

We, unlike Daniel, find ourselves in a time when we are eating a lot of meat and defending our names. The Spirit's work is to point the world to Jesus, not to us. Resisting culture looks much more like living simple, generous lives rather than voting for the right candidate or leading churches through best-practice business models.

In a culture so polarized by political views, we can get swept up in the debates, never noticing that the silent soul crusher of blaming and shaming others is nesting inside our hearts. In our culture, we often fight with our enemies instead of loving them, and we often adopt the weapons of rejection, and we can't pretend that our harsh rejection of people doesn't do damage. What if we instead wrapped ourselves in the towel of compassion and served our enemies in love?

If we are going to discover what it means to be the people of God now, we need to learn spiritual discernment. Our ability to discern will determine whether we find ourselves faithful in exile or consumed by Babylon.

Walking the Tightrope

This is why Lesslie Newbigin writes about the need for conversion in the church. If we are going to bear witness to Jesus, we first need to kneel before him, repenting collectively for how we have sinned. We need to have an open and honest talk with God, confessing our lack of love, repenting of our self-concern, and then trusting his Spirit to lead us moment by moment to show us the path to faithfulness.

A helpful way to picture discernment is to think of the gospel as a tightrope. The tightrope is suspended with the church on one side and the culture on the other. The way, the truth, and the life is the tightrope. If we fall off on the side of the church, we become separatists. We tend toward self-protection and sectarianism, fearful avoidance in our relationship with the culture in which we live.

To fall off in the other direction is to become syncretistic, meaning we affirm the culture's opinions and norms over Christ and Scripture. Falling off on this side makes us appear more culturally relevant, but we lack any distinction from the culture.

The only way to faithfulness is to keep coming back to the gospel for ourselves. Being the people of God is fundamentally a commitment to follow in the way, the truth, and the life of Jesus. Following Jesus doesn't mean we agree with the ideas of Jesus or what we might think Jesus thinks. It is a fundamental commitment to a relationship with him in which we submit to his teaching and model his life. It is an ongoing relationship that continually takes us deeper and deeper into his life and teaching, which simultaneously makes us more deeply engaged citizens and neighbors—citizens and neighbors willing to bless as well as resist. To stray from this commitment in either direction is sin. Period.

Which is why the people of God need continual conversion. We are always falling off on one side or the other. Claiming that we are a Baptist or a Lutheran and resting confidently in our church affiliation doesn't relieve our need for further conversion. Just because we affirm the culture's views on sexuality doesn't mean Jesus agrees with us. While falling off in one direction may mean we need to confess a lack of love, falling off on the other side may mean we have rejected Christ's teaching in some way that we need to repent of.

The best way to learn discernment is by inviting the Spirit of God to search our hearts and then confessing our sin to Jesus, who graciously receives us and forgives us.

Repentance is not a shameful act; it is a spiritual grace that Jesus gifts to his people. Faithfulness is not just the absence of sinning; it is also recognizing our sin and turning away from sin and to Christ in repentance. As the people of God in exile, we will need to be humble of soul and spirit because we have a lot to learn in this new world. The tightrope feels high, and the winds are blowing strong in both directions. There is pressure coming from the right and the left. But Jesus won't be blown over by Babylon, and if we are willing to keep reaching out our hands with every misstep, personally and collectively, we will find the strong grasp of an immovable King who is ready to keep us faithfully by his side.

SEVEN

Discovering the Rhythms of Grace through Spiritual Practices

Being the people of God in any time or place is demanding work. We have another kingdom, another King, and a deeper loyalty than the economy or the flag. However, in America, as in Babylon, to have a commitment above country is to be suspect of treasonous tendencies.

We stand spiritually with our immigrant neighbors, attesting that we are here but have another home, a deeper belonging and loyalty, a first language of faith and a second language of citizen.

The Muslim man at the bus stop in Portland makes me wonder what practicing faith looks like for God's people. If you remember, the man wore a long beard, a tunic-type robe, and

a small square cap on his head. His son wore a similar outfit, and his daughter's head was covered in a hijab. In a neighborhood filled with hipster beards and skinny jeans, this man and his children stood out in a striking way. It was clear from their appearance that they were practicing Muslims. What I found so striking was the way that practicing their faith was very much a part of their lives. From their clothing to the call to pray at a specific hour and toward a specific direction, practicing faith in the Muslim community has tangible distinctives.

That man continually comes to my mind and makes me think about my own faith. What are my practices? How does my faith in Christ lead me to distinct practices that differ from those of others in my city? My mind immediately goes to spending time in the Bible and prayer, but those are private and personal unless the sun is out or I am at a coffee shop. Thanks to my iPad, I no longer carry around a physical Bible, so even if I read the Bible in public, no one knows—unless I decide to read it out loud, but that is just obnoxious, regardless of what you are reading.

Next I think of my marriage. The fact that my wife, Jeanne, and I have been married faithfully to each other for twenty-eight years is a distinctive in our culture, but I have great friends with great marriages who have been married for about the same length of time, and they don't believe in Jesus.

I think of things I don't do most of the time, but the list doesn't make me a saint. I don't steal or go to strip clubs, but again, many people don't do those things and not because of any faith commitment on their part.

What I realize is that, for the most part, Christians don't have many spiritual practices that create public distinctiveness. We may attend church once a week, and if we are honest, it's more like twice a month, but the way we dress, work, shop, and live is pretty much like any other citizen in our communities. Then I think of the Israelites. Everything about their lives was connected to their faith and the story God had written them into. From the rhythms of work and rest to Sabbath and worship to their yearly calendar to how men shaved, everything was a part of a living practice that pointed to their story of being the people of God. While those were outward signs that didn't necessarily point to an inner faithfulness, the practices and rhythms were a means for their faith to be sustained in exile.

We live in a time when Christian faith and practice have been sequestered to the sphere of personal and private. As the Jews did, we struggle for an identity that is distinct as we live out our lives publicly and privately. This is a struggle that is not going away. In a real sense, this is a time when the church either discovers a new way of being in the world or is assimilated and forgotten.

It is time to put our faith into practice. *Practice* is the right word. It might seem like an odd word. We practice guitar, and athletes practice their sport. But doctors practice medicine and lawyers practice law and believers in Christ practice faith. The idea behind the word *practice* is that we are engaged in applying what we believe and know in real-life situations. In this case, the situation is life.

Reimagining Faith

In exile, the Israelites practiced their faith in their God. Some of those practices were as old as Moses, but they also found new ways of practicing their faith in a new world. Those practices achieved two things for the community's formation in exile.

First, their practices preserved their identity as the people of God.

Babylon had a powerful cultural force, and the empire was highly religious in its practices. The exiled Jews found themselves in an entirely foreign land with foreign gods. Everything from the food to the clothing to the calendar was different from what they had known. Collectively practicing their common faith in this new and uncommon world preserved their identity as distinct from Babylon and the Babylonian way of life. Without discovering a new way to practice faithfulness, the people of God would have disappeared in Babylon, slowly assimilated into the culture until their distinct identity as God's chosen people disappeared altogether.

Second, God's people were sustained by their practices.

Life in Babylon, not unlike life in any empire, was soul crushing. Their new world created anxiety and offered fleeting relief through pleasures of the flesh. It would have been easy to simply be assimilated into the values and customs of the new world, but the Israelites found through daily and weekly rhythms that they could be an alternative community sustained by God, who is always with and for his people. They would also have an opportunity to give witness to the deeper and more meaningful life of peace that Babylon, despite all her glory, could never truly provide.

Babylon was a nation of economic and military power and force. In Babylon, the Darwinian motto "Eat or be eaten" was alive and well. Israel told a better story than Babylon did. The Israelites had a Creator God who made humans to work in partnership with him so that humanity could flourish. He invited his people to stop and celebrate once a week and to remember that they were not God and that the world was held together even when they slept. This God called his people to live in such a way that everyone would flourish, not just the upper classes. Love was the mark of neighborliness, and as a result, their homes were places to make peace as well as bread.

Their faith practices pointed them to the larger story of their God, who was still at work and in charge even as they lived away from their homeland in captivity. Their faith practices also pointed those outside their community to an alternative God, an alternative story, and an alternative way of life that could be tasted, appreciated, and believed in.

If the Israelites had not practiced their faith collectively and publicly, their Torah would soon have collected dust on the shelf and their way of life would have subtly but powerfully been assimilated into the way of life in Babylon.

That didn't happen. Despite the dominating forces nationally and culturally, Babylon could not assimilate the Israelites. And it wasn't for a lack of trying. The Babylonians tried and failed to assimilate the people of God. And it wasn't because the Israelites were so good either. They sinned and disobeyed God throughout the Old Testament. But they were carried through by the grace of God and an intentional way of practicing their faith that sustained them individually and collectively and pointed anyone willing to look to a God more glorious than the gods of Babylon.

The Power of Practicing Faith Now

Life in twenty-first-century America is exhausting with its speed of change, pace of life, and demands of education, work, and relationships. Even thinking about having to practice something else is enough to make you close this book right now. Trying to add anything to our plate is enough to push us over the edge. America, like Babylon, is full of pressure and pleasures. Many of us rely on God just to make it through the day.

Unknowingly, we have accepted the word on the street as our story. The concept of "Eat or be eaten" was a line that was fed to us, and we have believed it. Jesus is walled off into a compartment in our minds that we access to find the energy and the patience we need to keep up with the Kardashians. Too many of us are exhausted from the pressures of the empire, and we find ourselves binging on its pleasures to short-circuit the anxiety we feel, even if those pleasures are only a temporary fix. I believe Jesus intended more for us and more from us when he promised that we would have life and have it more abundantly (John 10:10).

Recovering a way of practicing our faith in both public and private, individually and collectively, will have the same preserving, sustaining, and life-giving effect that it did for the Israelites in exile. The power of God is no less ours today than it was theirs. The promises of God are just as true for us as they were for them, but the way we apply them and put them into practice can powerfully reshape how we engage our faith and enter into public spaces as followers of Jesus.

In the next several chapters, I will introduce five practices. They are biblical and have the power to form our souls in the face of the pressures of exile. They also enable us to bear witness to the gospel of Christ in ways that both bless our neighbors and resist the powerful culture that seeks to assimilate us. Resisting Babylon through these practices becomes prophetic when we tell a different story with our lives, a story that points to Jesus, who is King over all things. These practices are meant to set us free from Babylon's power and to help us experience life in deep and meaningful ways. Faithfulness is freedom for those who follow Jesus.

The intention behind these practices is not to create something else for us to add to our lives. Instead, these practices are meant to help us turn around and fully enter the story of God in our everyday lives.

By turning around (repentance) and seeing that everything we are doing is already a part of God's story, we can adjust our focus and our energy to experience the freedom God has for us in that story and his power to sustain us in Babylon.

My daughter loves the Narnia stories. C. S. Lewis used fantasy to capture reality. The wardrobe served as the entrance into a larger story and a deeper magic. Outside the wardrobe, the Pevensie children were living ordinary lives as typical schoolkids, but once they walked through the wardrobe, they were kings and queens, stewarding and ruling in the midst of a cosmic battle between good and evil. Inside the wardrobe was a deeper reality that Lewis used to help us imagine the spiritual world in which we are living and the deeper story to which we belong.

The people of God both live and tell an alternative story, a story that rests its hope on our sovereign and saving God, in whom our hopes and allegiances find their footing. Faith is the hardest part, because it requires that we come to trust that the story of Jesus is the center of reality. Jesus's story is more real than what is streaming on Netflix this month. God uses the ordinary experiences of time, money, eating, and work to fill the large space in our lives between Sundays. He allows us to be both a faithful presence and a prophetic

FAITH FOR THIS MOMENT

witness while being sustained and formed by his Word and Spirit. We can see the power and the sacredness of what we are giving ourselves to, and he redeems our ordinary activities by weaving them into his story and making us participants in his purposes. Freedom has a special fragrance, as we become the aroma of life to the world around us.

In the chapters that follow, we will explore five practices that are meant to help us remember and participate in the story of God. The centering practice, to which all the others are connected, is to hear and obey. When we have an underlying commitment to hear God's Word and to listen to the Holy Spirit with the intention of obeying what we have heard, our posture changes from that of a spectator to that of a participant. The other four practices overlap one another in an interconnected pattern that weaves itself through our lives. Hospitality, generosity, Sabbath, and vocation intersect with most areas of our lives. If we intentionally and worshipfully give ourselves to Jesus in these areas of our lives, the dynamic that occurs is transformational. The power of Babylon gets broken, and the power of Christ breaks in.

Freedom in Babylon

Our lives were not meant to be an exhausted, frantic, anxiety-filled grind. Life in Jesus has a sacredness to it, a rhythm that beats to the ways of grace. If we are taking our cues from Babylon, then we get used up. Life becomes small and we feel used. Life in Christ is the opposite. Life is a large canvas on which Christ paints his beauty of salvation. Our work is as holy as our Bible reading. Our table is a sacred place for eating and sharing life. What we do with our time and money tells a story of freedom or slavery. When we stop working, turn off our devices, and become human again, we adamantly testify that we will not be reduced to a machine. When we create space to worship Jesus in a collective community of exiles, we find our way of being in the meal of bread and wine. Whatever we practice tells a story of what our lives are being lived for.

If you were to look back at the past week, paying attention to how you spent your time, where you ate your meals and who you ate them with, what you gave your money and energy to, and if you created space to rest and worship, what story would it tell about who you are and who your God is? Being honest, most of us would have to admit that our week told pretty much the same story as that of any other person living for the American dream. God has a better story he wants to tell through our lives.

The centering practice that holds all the others together is to hear and obey. I am convinced that if we get this one right, the others will fall into place. That's what we are going to look at next.

EIGHT

The Centering Practice

I love to read. For years, I hated to read fiction. I immersed myself in books that gave me what I deemed meaningful information that I could use in everyday life. I would buy a novel, read it for an hour—all the while looking at the thickness of the book and how slowly the pages were turning and how many were left to be turned—and eventually put it down and pick up a different book without all the fluff of character and plot.

Something in me shifted awhile back. I found myself drawn to good stories. We have an emotional response to the words "Once upon a time . . . " that draws us into a world of possibilities. Maybe the years of trying and failing to put into practice all the useful things I had read or maybe the fact that I was getting older made me more open to stories. I found myself drawn into other worlds that helped me reflect on my own world.

There is nothing like getting into a book that you can't put down. The hours fly by as you lose yourself in the

well-written prose. Story is the main genre that God uses to reveal himself to us, and I think that is because we are somehow emotionally hardwired to learn through the immersive experience of finding ourselves in a story that is worth reading.

The Story We Are In

Babylon is the metaphor we are using to help us understand life in this new world of exile. We are trying to answer the question, What does it mean to be the people of God now? Every culture is formed by a narrative. Babylon had a story, and the United States has a story. The narrative is powerful. It can form and inform our understanding of ourselves, our place in the world, who our neighbors are, what we think about them, and who our enemies are. This story can shape what we think about love and life.

But God also has a story. He gave us the Scriptures and primarily used the form of story to reveal himself to us. The people of God are participants in God's story, and when we begin to organize our lives around God's story and not Babylon's, we find freedom from the destructive and anxiety-inducing narrative of Babylon.

When all is said and done, we organize our lives around a particular story. What story are you organizing your life around?

What do you think about yourself and your future?

What do you think about work?

What did you spend your time on this week?

What does your bank account express about what you believe?

We are all formed by stories because we organize our lives around them. Our lives are telling a story, so what story are they telling?

Journey into the Story of God

Have you ever read through the Bible cover to cover? A few years back at my church, we taught through the Bible in a year. We hit most of the books, one book a week. Week after week, home communities and small groups read through the Bible together.

The Bible is a long book, no question about that, but when we read it from cover to cover, we hear it in a fresh way. Reading the story of God from Genesis to Revelation allows us to catch the larger themes of the biblical story. We catch glimpses of salvation coming to God's people. Sin and redemption wash over the pages at every point in the story. These themes are not accidental; they weave a narrative in which every person on earth is invited to participate. God desires for everyone to be a participant and no one to be a spectator.

For the people of God, the story of Scripture is the anchoring story for our lives and our understanding of the world around us. Scripture defines who we are and shapes our understanding of life. Most importantly, it reveals to us the God who has come to us in Christ.

But the Bible has fallen on hard times as of late. Perhaps this is happening because for too many years people treated the Scriptures like a religious textbook instead of the holy Word of God. Whatever the cause, when it comes to God's Word, most of us aren't listening.

Information Doesn't Lead to Transformation

The modern educational system was built on a premise of mastery rather than practice. We go to school, learn information, and after we have mastered a given field, we go and participate in that field. We come, we grow, and then we go.

That is not how Jesus trained his disciples. His was a school of apprenticeship in which what people learned was put into practice the day they learned it.

The philosophy of learning that we have in our school systems was also adopted by the church. The experience goes something like this: we go to church, we grow in our faith, and one day when we have it all figured out, we go out and serve faithfully. The lie embedded in this well-meaning model of discipleship is this: information leads to transformation. We believe that the more information we acquire, the more we will be transformed into a great practitioner. We become paralyzed thinking we don't have enough information, enough mastery, or enough training to participate in God's purposes.

All of this has given rise to the paralyzing question, How? This is a question of avoidance. If we claim we don't understand and don't know how to do something, and we do this long enough, perhaps people will quit expecting much from us, including Jesus.

Our claims of ignorance were only helped along by the professionalization of pastors. As pastors acquired seminary degrees, a chasm was created between the paid leaders and the congregation. The largest and most damaging effect was that God's people started believing they could hear God's voice from Scripture only if a trained professional who had studied the original languages explained it to them.

The results have been devastating, and that is not an exaggeration. People put down their Bibles and picked up how-to books. Believing that what they lacked was information, and trusting the lie that information leads to transformation, believers were left waiting for the next book, the next program, the next delivery system that would give them the right information about God. They believed that by the time they finished the latest book, they would be masters in the life of faith. But countless books stacked up on the shelves of well-intentioned believers, while our lives remained pretty much the same.

Now in exile, we are always looking for a way out. Babylon is exhausting, and we are all searching for meaning and something more. So we wait for the next big thing that will teach us how to master this thing of faith.

But waiting to figure out "how to" leads to a long life of apathy and puts off participation in God's story right now.

Participation Leads to Transformation

Among God's people, everyone is a participant and no one is a spectator.

The answer we are looking for is found in the posture of our hearts, not the information in our heads.

Jesus gives this invitation in Matthew's Gospel:

Are you tired? Worn out? Burned out on religion? Come to me. Get away with me and you'll recover your life. I'll show you how to take a real rest. Walk with me and work with me—watch how I do it. Learn the unforced rhythms of grace. I won't lay anything heavy or ill-fitting on you. Keep company with me and you'll learn to live freely and lightly. (11:28–30 Message)

Jesus's invitation is to be his apprentice in this life. We don't lack information; in fact, we don't lack anything. Being an apprentice of Jesus is simply a matter of practicing a new way of listening to his voice. His promise is that his way is an easy yoke and a light burden. In Babylon, everything comes by force. Labor forces, military forces, and the forces of the economy all leave us burned out and burdened. But Jesus invites us into a life of "unforced rhythms of grace."

Adopting a new set of practices is not about learning new skills. We allow God to transform ordinary things that we are already doing—such as working, eating, spending, and being a neighbor—by letting his story shape how we practice those things. Essentially, we are turning toward the grace that Jesus has for us right now in this minute and allowing that grace to seep in and transform the ordinary, everyday stuff of living.

I believe that what gives followers of Jesus distinction in Babylon is the subversive way we do the ordinary things of life. Instead of finding the right candidate for president, we can resist the empire of Babylon more powerfully by finding the right candidate to invite to dinner. That may sound like nonsense to us, but for some reason it didn't to Jesus. He was more concerned with the woman at the well than the king on the throne.

This is the revolution of God's people in exile. We bless and resist the world in which we live when the shape of our lives is formed by hearing and obeying God's Word. We simply need to get away with Jesus and listen to his voice.

Turning toward the grace that is already present in our lives means letting go of the lie that information leads to transformation and trusting that all Jesus requires is that we listen to him and obey him. The Holy Spirit is the one who grants the power, but our intention matters. As we turn toward the grace that Jesus has already given us, this turning requires that we put to death the idea of "come, grow, and go" and replace it with "hear and obey." We quit asking how and start seeking Jesus.

I love the following story in Mark's Gospel. Here was a guy who was literally destroying himself. He was in anguish spiritually and mentally, and all anyone could do for him was tie him down so he didn't harm himself. After Jesus healed him, Mark tells us what happened:

> As Jesus was getting into the boat, the man who had been demon-possessed begged to go with him. Jesus did not let him, but said, "Go home to your own people and tell them how much the Lord has done for you, and how he has had mercy on you." So the man went away and began to tell in the Decapolis how much Jesus had done for him. And all the people were amazed. (5:18–20)

This man, who will be forever known as the demoniac, which is not a name that most of us would choose for ourselves, had no training or education in the ways of God from what we are told. He didn't even get to follow Jesus for a single day. When he asked to follow Jesus, Jesus told him no. Instead, he sent him to his hometown to tell the people all that God had done for him. What did he do? He didn't give all the reasons he wasn't ready for a mission trip. He didn't talk about the past several years and his need to spend time in a small group first. No, he just went.

Later, when Jesus entered that region of the Ten Cities, the crowds were huge. People came out to see Jesus because they knew what Jesus had done for this man. How did they know? Because the man had done what Jesus had told him to do. He listened and obeyed.

Hearing and Obeying Has Always Been Our Practice

Throughout the Bible, we never see the idea of "come, grow, and go." Instead, we see over and over that the people of God were to hear and obey God, and this led to the path of life. Hearing and obeying were not about having all the information but about having the right posture of the heart.

In both the Old and the New Testament, the people of God were commanded to hear and obey the Word of God at the center of their lives. We see this when Moses instructed the people of God in Deuteronomy:

> Hear, O Israel: The LORD our God, the LORD is one. Love the LORD your God with all your heart and with all your soul and with all your strength. These commandments that I give you today are to be on your hearts. Impress them on your children. Talk about them when you sit at home and when you walk along the road, when you lie down and when you get up. Tie them as symbols on your hands and bind them on your foreheads. Write them on the doorframes of your houses and on your gates. (6:4–9)

Hearing and obeying God's Word formed the people spiritually, creating an alternative community in the world. This community would bless the world as well as resist its godless ways. God's people were to form a community that loved God and loved one another.

The practice of hearing and obeying also sustained and preserved God's people as they experienced many forms and times of exile throughout their history. God knew what lay ahead of them, and he equipped them for a future when they would experience exile. His instructions were given centuries before, in the book of Deuteronomy. Hearing and obeying would be the way God's people survived the hostile conditions that threatened their faith.

> Be careful, or you will be enticed to turn away and worship other gods and bow down to them. Then the LORD's anger will burn against you, and he will shut up the heavens so that it will not rain and the ground will yield no produce, and you will soon perish from the good land the LORD is giving you. Fix these words of mine in your hearts and minds; tie them as symbols on your hands and bind them on your foreheads. Teach them to your children, talking about them when you sit at home and when you walk along the road, when you lie down and when you get up. Write them on the doorframes of your houses and on your gates, so that your days and the days of your children may be many in the land the LORD swore to give your ancestors, as many as the days that the heavens are above the earth. (Deut. 11:16–21)

God is the speaker. He speaks his ways, his thoughts, his nature, and his love to us. We are the listeners, with hearts open and attentive to receive what he has to say to us and ready to respond and put it into practice.

The question is, Do we trust his Word? God has promised to be our God and that we will be his people. We are the people of God, and therefore his words to us are meant to give life, not to harm or destroy. God will never use us like Babylon uses us. He calls us sons and daughters who get to participate with their Father in his purposes. Trusting his grace and goodness allows us to live a better story than Babylon will ever tell.

Jesus Helps Us Hear and Obey

"Therefore everyone who hears these words of mine and puts them into practice is like a wise man who built his house on the rock. The rain came down, the streams rose, and the winds blew and beat against that house; yet it did not fall, because it had its foundation on the rock. But everyone who hears these words of mine and does not put them into practice is like a foolish man who built his house on sand. The rain came down, the streams rose, and the winds blew and beat against that house, and it fell with a great crash."

When Jesus had finished saying these things, the crowds were amazed at his teaching, because he taught as one who had authority, and not as their teachers of the law. (Matt. 7:24–29)

Hear what Jesus says here.
Not hear and consider.
Not hear and analyze.
Not hear and deliberate.
Hear and obey.
Hear these words and put them into practice. The picture Jesus painted couldn't have been clearer. A house built on sand is no match for the storms that swirl through Babylon. If we are formed by our culture's story and build our lives on

the promises of our cultural moment, then we are building our lives on sand.

The same is true if we acknowledge God's words as true but never put them into practice. If we hear but never obey, we are on shaky ground. We are in the same predicament as those who never heard Jesus's words at all, only we are seen as fools who knew the importance of building on the rock but chose the sand instead.

Hearing and obeying sounds difficult, but Jesus said it is easy. With so many competing stories, we are bound to feel as if we are missing some wonderful Babylonian promises. Everyone around us seems to be getting in on the action. Left to ourselves, we must put forth an extraordinary effort to hear and obey.

But Jesus said it is easy!

How can that be?

Hearing and obeying is easy because Jesus gives us the grace we need as we turn toward him. To hear and obey is to point our lives toward the grace of Jesus and let him order our way. The turning takes effort, the trusting seems counterintuitive, but once we get a taste of life that is truly life, turning to Jesus to hear and obey grows into a new way of being, a new way to be the people of God in exile.

To Bless and Resist

God envisioned that he would have an alternative community of people who belonged to him in a world that had been hijacked by spiritual and national powers. In the midst of many dark stories, a people who lived the story of God would be a light in the darkness. Their life together would speak to a goodness and a beauty that people living out the dark stories would long for. As a result, the people of God would be a blessing to the world around them. In the surrounding stories of death, they would tell a story of life.

That alternative story would also be a prophetic one. Life together for the people of God would push back and critique other narratives. The way God's people practiced faithfulness, neighborliness, holiness, and grace would serve as a natural critique of the self-centered, self-serving stories of Babylon. This community, through hearing and obeying, would be both a faithful presence of God in the world and a prophetic witness of the ways the world had gone sideways. This community would be a city on a hill and a light in the darkness.

Hearing and Obeying

Hearing and obeying God is the centering practice that informs and shapes all the other practices. It can take many forms.

Holy Listening

When we open our Bibles or our Bible apps, the words are the words of God. Our job is to open our ears and our hearts to the message. We aren't reading a textbook, dissecting it for information. There is a lot to learn, and study can be a powerful thing, but for the purpose of this practice, we lay aside the need to become theological experts. We are interested in listening to Holy Scripture and humbly allowing the Word to wash over us and through us. Holy listening is the practice of attuning ourselves to God's voice. We submit ourselves to God's Word as God's people.

Collective Listening

The people of God are an interdependent community. When we listen to Scripture together, we hear it in a larger capacity. More ears, more listening. We listen in small groups, we listen with friends, and we listen as a congregation. As we hear God's Word together, we are able to discern together what obedience looks like. We discern collectively what it means to obey, and we help each other to hear and obey. Doing so may mean helping a teacher discern how they can bless their classroom by being a faithful presence to their students or helping a businessperson discern how to resist the corporate diminishing of their holy work. We listen together so we can obey together. We carry each other through the streets of exile in collective community.

Listening Prayer

We also listen to the Spirit of God at work in our lives through prayer. We learn to hear by paying attention to our lives, our relationships, our wounds, and our joys. A professor I had once said that God gave us two ears and one mouth. Prayer should be more listening than speaking. Alone and together we can hear the Spirit's movements in our lives and discern his invitations to deeper faithfulness.

A Way of Life

There is no magic program for hearing God's Word and obeying it. The practice is simple but profound. Throughout the week, we find times to place our lives under God's Word personally and with others. We do this with the intent to respond to what we have heard. We repent when needed, turning from the ways of Babylon toward the God who gives us life and sustains us by his Word. We listen to obey, not to debate.

We won't get the practice right all the time. That is why it's called a practice. We have to keep at it to develop the appropriate habits, attitudes, and postures. Over time, hearing and obeying will become our way of life. We will find ourselves changing. Faith that once was a set of beliefs that we acknowledged will become a living thing. As our lifeline in exile, hearing and obeying will shape our desires and choices. We will become distinct as the people of God, as Israel was distinct in the midst of Babylon.

NINE

Hospitality

Imagine that you have just arrived at a party. The invitation you received a couple weeks earlier assured you that it was going to be a great night and that everyone invited wanted to have you with them. The intimate dinner was for eight to ten people, all of whom you had met but were mostly just acquaintances.

As you park the car, you feel a bit of nerves in your stomach. At the door, you can hear the guests laughing and getting to know one another over drinks and hors d'oeuvres. You knock on the door. They keep talking. You wait a minute and knock again. Still no answer—not even a pause in the conversation.

Finally, you turn the handle and let yourself in. Once in, no one even notices you. The host walks right by you while you stand there holding your coat.

Those first few minutes tell you that you don't want to be there. Now there is the dilemma. Do you stay or do you go?

Can you sneak out without anyone noticing? You assume so because they haven't really noticed you yet.

Most of us know the power of being unwelcome. The awkward predicament that being unwelcome puts us in has the power to make us want to disappear.

But being welcome can also have a profound impact on us. The simplicity of a smile and hearing "I'm so glad you're here" shapes our self-understanding. Being welcome is the foundation of experiencing hospitality.

Inhospitable Empires

Ancient cultures understood that their willingness to be hospitable to strangers was a sign of a moral civilization.

In 2016, we witnessed the worst humanitarian crisis of our time. The United Nations identified 13.5 million people needing humanitarian assistance. Almost 7 million people were displaced inside Syria and another 4.8 million outside the country in the wake of a civil war. The world watched as refugees fought for their lives, hoping to get to hospitable shores. The nations of the world struggled to find a response. Many closed their borders, unwilling to allow people in, fearing that terrorists may be embedded among the refugees. Most settled in Eastern countries of Turkey, Lebanon, Jordan, Iraq, and Egypt. Roughly 1.3 million requested asylum in Europe. Between the years 2011 and 2016, the United States admitted only eighteen thousand Syrian refugees.[1]

Modern-day Babylon is not a hospitable place. It is not surprising that the nations of the East mentioned above received almost 5 million of the refugees who had been displaced.

Eastern countries still carry within them the ancient customs of hospitality.

National security and the reality of the war on terror are legitimate concerns for any nation. The atrocities that occurred in Syria, and the aftermath of death and displacement, conflicted with the security concerns of Western countries, leaving an ethical conundrum that gave rise to heated debate. Rhetoric was high, as were tensions, but a willingness to act on behalf of these vulnerable people, many of whom were children, was sadly too late in many cases.

Babylon is suspicious by nature. The stranger and the foreigner are most often seen as enemies and threats rather than as people who bear the image of God. As a result, our countries and our communities have become unwelcoming. Our homes are less hospitable than they once were, and even our neighborhoods tend to be insular, if not gated.

Hospitality is not without its concerns, and yet the people of God are called to practice hospitality even in the inhospitable conditions of exile.

Hospitality and the People of God

Today we easily believe that our security and wealth are deserved rather than a privilege we experience and extend to others, and suspicion of the outsider is high. But God wants us to get in touch with our own otherness and stranger status. As it was for Israel, hospitality for the church is grounded in a personal understanding that we are welcomed by God even though we are foreigners and strangers to him.

For Israel, the hospitality commands came out of their own history of slavery under Pharaoh's empire. The harsh treatment and conditions that they endured under the powerful regime reduced them to servitude and sought to destroy their human dignity.

God, however, had other plans. Not only did he restore their dignity, but he also called them to extend human dignity and welcome to those who found themselves in similar conditions:

> When a foreigner resides among you in your land, do not mistreat them. The foreigner residing among you must be treated as your native-born. Love them as yourself, for you were foreigners in Egypt. I am the LORD your God. (Lev. 19:33–34)

Israel's history allowed them to see the stranger and the other not as a threat but as one of them.

God took hospitality among his people very seriously because a willingness to welcome those who were far off revealed his very heart to the world. Unlike the surrounding nations, Israel was to express an alternative story concerning the issues of security and self-protection. They were to speak of the welcoming God in a way that all the world could hear.

The New Testament community understood their spiritual identity as both being welcomed by God and being strangers in the world, exiles in Babylon at home with the Father, Son, and Spirit. They knew they were not at home in the world but had received a gracious welcome into God's home.

> Consequently, you are no longer foreigners and strangers, but fellow citizens with God's people and also members of his household, built on the foundation of the apostles and

prophets, with Christ Jesus himself as the chief cornerstone. In him the whole building is joined together and rises to become a holy temple in the Lord. And in him you too are being built together to become a dwelling in which God lives by his Spirit. (Eph. 2:19–22)

Our spiritual experience of being far off but welcomed graciously by God empowers us to welcome those we would consider the stranger, the foreigner, and the other. We find freedom in this practice of extending a loving welcome to the other because we have received a similar welcome from the Father, Son, and Spirit.

Jesus radicalized the practice of hospitality by telling his disciples that when they welcomed the "least of these" in the world, they were actually welcoming him. The command to practice hospitality to strangers is an invitation to participate in a sacred type of communion in which we see Jesus in the face of the other and welcome his presence into our lives, in the tangible space of our homes.

The writer of Hebrews carried this theme even further when he said, "Keep on loving one another as brothers and sisters. Do not forget to show hospitality to strangers, for by so doing some people have shown hospitality to angels without knowing it" (13:1–2).

Obstacles to Hospitality Abound

The conditions we are living in are inhospitable. Everyone's suspicions are high. After 9/11, the world changed forever. Terrorism is meant to do one thing: terrorize. Often Christians respond to these inhospitable conditions by becoming suspicious of people who are different from us. Hospitality in an era of terrorism seems foolish to many Christians.

Even if we don't fear the stranger, we rarely have time for other people in the busyness of our daily lives. If we are honest, we barely have time to be with those we call friends, let alone strangers. As creatures of habit, we tend to associate with people who are like us, be it through race, class, or the type of music we listen to. We tend to trade community for affinity and remain satisfied in our comfort.

God's often-repeated commands to practice hospitality can appear shortsighted and foolish at worst and irritating and uncomfortable at best.

God knows, however, that the path to life is not in self-protection and affinity. Because he is good and life-giving, he invites us to hear and obey his invitation to hospitality, knowing it will transform both the one who offers the welcome and the one who is welcomed.

Overcoming Affinity with Hospitality

Jesus was great at making people uncomfortable. He picked a band of twelve disciples who didn't have much in common. He hung out with religious people and the people with whom religious folks would never associate. Everywhere he went he broke down the false security of affinity and invited people into a deeper human community with one another. Listen to this story from the Gospel of Luke:

> Then Jesus said to his host, "When you give a luncheon or dinner, do not invite your friends, your brothers or sisters, your relatives, or your rich neighbors; if you do, they may

invite you back and so you will be repaid. But when you give a banquet, invite the poor, the crippled, the lame, the blind, and you will be blessed. Although they cannot repay you, you will be repaid at the resurrection of the righteous." (14:12–14)

When we throw parties for our friends, Jesus wouldn't call that hospitality. For Jesus, the word was full of meaning about our common humanity, and he wasn't going to let it be reduced to affinity.

At the center of true hospitality is a willingness to serve another without expecting repayment, to love selflessly with no expectation of a return on our investment. Opening up a couple of seats at your table for people who are different from you the next time you throw a dinner party is a good place to start. Invite a few people who don't share your race, your age, or your beliefs. Treat them as you would your closest friend. Create space where they are valued and given the status of friend, not stranger. Watch what God does in your heart and around your table as a deeper and richer community is created before your eyes. Replacing affinity with a more authentic community is the fruit of hospitality. Practicing hospitality opens the door to our own transformation and announces to an insecure world that human love and dignity will not be found in building bigger fences.

The Problem with "Nice"

Jesus was in many ways disruptive at parties. In other words, he didn't make the nicest guest. He was uncivil at times and ignored many of the manners and customs of his day. We see that vividly in this story from Luke 7:

When one of the Pharisees invited Jesus to have dinner with him, he went to the Pharisee's house and reclined at the table. A woman in that town who lived a sinful life learned that Jesus was eating at the Pharisee's house, so she came there with an alabaster jar of perfume. As she stood behind him at his feet weeping, she began to wet his feet with her tears. Then she wiped them with her hair, kissed them and poured perfume on them.

When the Pharisee who had invited him saw this, he said to himself, "If this man were a prophet, he would know who is touching him and what kind of woman she is—that she is a sinner."

Jesus answered him, "Simon, I have something to tell you."

"Tell me, teacher," he said.

"Two people owed money to a certain moneylender. One owed him five hundred denarii, and the other fifty. Neither of them had the money to pay him back, so he forgave the debts of both. Now which of them will love him more?"

Simon replied, "I suppose the one who had the bigger debt forgiven."

"You have judged correctly," Jesus said.

Then he turned toward the woman and said to Simon, "Do you see this woman? I came into your house. You did not give me any water for my feet, but she wet my feet with her tears and wiped them with her hair. You did not give me a kiss, but this woman, from the time I entered, has not stopped kissing my feet. You did not put oil on my head, but she has poured perfume on my feet. Therefore, I tell you, her many sins have been forgiven—as her great love has shown. But whoever has been forgiven little loves little."

Then Jesus said to her, "Your sins are forgiven."

The other guests began to say among themselves, "Who is this who even forgives sins?"

Jesus said to the woman, "Your faith has saved you; go in peace." (vv. 36–50)

Jesus was willing to be an uncivil, impolite guest. He had no problem disrupting the nice, sentimental hospitality of the Pharisees. He offered true hospitality, with its life-changing welcome, to an uninvited guest right in the middle of a perfectly good dinner party.

Hospitality is not about being nice. It acknowledges the harsh realities of life in Babylon. It mends the wounded and pardons the guilty. It goes the extra mile to get into the messy pain of another person's life and sits with them there waiting for God. It welcomes whole people, wounds and all. Hospitality that both blesses and resists tells the truth about what and who really matter. Hospitality doesn't always look like a party, but it causes rejoicing in the souls of strangers and in the heart of God.

Practicing Hospitality

What makes the people of God both a blessing and a resisting presence in exile is the willingness to replace the culture's definition of hospitality with that of Jesus. While we would love to be invited to the Governor's Ball, Jesus is happy to be a guest who is served tacos in the barrio by undocumented people who are working to squeeze out an existence for their families.

In exile, God's people are willing to give up privacy and security and exchange them for welcoming vulnerability. Risking our personal comfort and even security is no more a risk today than it was in the Old Testament. Many of God's people have slept with one eye open at night as they provided shelter and food for those who were seeking it. Perhaps we can learn, as many others have, that most of the time the stranger becomes the gift God gives us to break down the idols of self-protection and personal security. Only when we risk our own comfort by opening our lives to the stranger can we experience the value of the sacred welcome we have received from Christ.

The skills needed to practice hospitality are pretty simple. Start with a simple meal and extend an invitation. Rather than trying to impress your guests, focus on loving and knowing them. Reach out to someone you don't know very well. Include people who are different from you. Be willing to bring hospitality to someone in need. A meal for a sick coworker or a few hours cleaning their house provides a welcome that you bring with you into their space.

Practicing hospitality makes us aware of God and draws us into our relationship with him, because at the heart of the practice lies a spiritual reality that we all share. We were strangers who were far off, alienated from God and broken by Babylon and our choices, but God came near. He welcomed us. If we are going to get this practice right, we need to keep in mind our own stranger-guest status with God. Being grateful and always remembering that we were strangers whom God welcomed as guests help us to see the stranger among us as being worthy of God's welcome. Jesus described this welcome in John's Gospel: "Anyone who loves me will obey my teaching. My Father will love them, and we will come to them and make our home with them" (14:23).

God moved into our lives and became our host, welcoming us into his life as he made his home in ours. Any understanding of this at the most basic level should move us to extend a similar grace to others.

At the same time, God also made himself a stranger in need of hospitality. He left the security of heaven to enter the inhospitable conditions of broken Babylon. He opened himself up to needing to be welcomed: "Those whom I love I rebuke and discipline. So be earnest and repent. Here I am! I stand at the door and knock. If anyone hears my voice and opens the door, I will come in and eat with that person, and they with me" (Rev. 3:19–20).

The practice of hospitality is one of the most revolutionary practices in which the people of God can participate. In a world of self-protection, God's people can bless Babylon with a welcome and refuse to see the stranger as a problem to avoid. Rather, we can welcome the stranger as though they were Jesus himself. Love flows from God through his people in order to announce to others that even in exile we will welcome them just as God has welcomed us.

TEN

Generosity

Babylon, like all empires, was ruled by wealth. Class systems built on race and nobility were the norm for ancient empires, as was the constant striving to acquire wealth for the empire and for personal gain. In America, the economy is king. Capitalism is built on supply and demand, buying and selling. Opportunity is available for anyone regardless of race, class, or gender, but the system favors the rich and the privileged. While many poor people pull themselves up and out of poverty, most can't find a way out, and too many slip down the rungs of the economic ladder—and off the rungs altogether.

In our modern-day Babylon, the motto "Everyone for himself" fits the bill. The practice of generosity is antithetical to this capitalistic motto. Money is a powerful thing, and God has always known that money has the power to wrap itself around our hearts and choke the divine life of the Spirit right out of us.

The God of Abundance

This is why the Israelites were called to model life free from the fear of scarcity, trusting in a God who provides abundantly. God foresaw long ago that when his community of emancipated slaves entered into a land flowing with milk and honey, they would be susceptible to the type of self-made success that causes people to make an idol out of the things they accumulate and sets them up to be prideful and arrogant. God warned his people about the temptation surrounding life in a wealthy land:

> For the LORD your God is bringing you into a good land—a land with brooks, streams, and deep springs gushing out into the valleys and hills; a land with wheat and barley, vines and fig trees, pomegranates, olive oil and honey; a land where bread will not be scarce and you will lack nothing; a land where the rocks are iron and you can dig copper out of the hills.
>
> When you have eaten and are satisfied, praise the LORD your God for the good land he has given you. Be careful that you do not forget the LORD your God, failing to observe his commands, his laws and his decrees that I am giving you this day. Otherwise, when you eat and are satisfied, when you build fine houses and settle down, and when your herds and flocks grow large and your silver and gold increase and all you have is multiplied, then your heart will become proud and you will forget the LORD your God, who brought you out of Egypt, out of the land of slavery. (Deut. 8:7–14)

Knowing that wealth can cause spiritual amnesia, God warned about the deceptive powers of nice things.

God often warned his people that wealth and prosperity could lead them to forget who they were and what God had done for them. Perhaps the harshest of God's judgments against Israel as a nation was that their own self-interest and greed drove them to take advantage of lower-class people and as a result brought disorder to God's dream of harmony among his chosen people. Instead of loving their neighbors, they began exploiting them. Not only did they lack generosity, but they also violently attacked the concept altogether through arrogant consumption. In short, they did anything to save a buck. When we are willing to take advantage of others to get a better deal, and we do so without regret, we have bought ourselves a ticket into exile.

People matter to God. The desire to accumulate wealth often leads to the exploitation of people who matter to God. When we forget our own poverty before God, we quickly forget the poor who live among us. What is worse, we may even exploit the poor and find ourselves at war with the God who is their protector. We see this warning throughout the Bible. Literally hundreds of verses show us that a lack of generosity sets us on a road to exploitive behavior. Here are just a few:

> He executes justice for the fatherless and the widow, and loves the sojourner, giving him food and clothing. (Deut. 10:18 ESV)

> For there will never cease to be poor in the land. Therefore I command you, "You shall open wide your hand to your brother, to the needy and to the poor, in your land." (Deut. 15:11 ESV)

> You would shame the plans of the poor,
> but the LORD is his refuge. (Ps. 14:6 ESV)

Whoever is generous to the poor lends to the LORD,
and he will repay him for his deed.
(Prov. 19:17 ESV)

When the poor and needy seek water,
and there is none,
and their tongue is parched with thirst,
I the LORD will answer them;
I the God of Israel will not forsake them.
(Isa. 41:17 ESV)

Behold, this was the guilt of your sister Sodom: she and her daughters had pride, excess of food, and prosperous ease, but did not aid the poor and needy. (Ezek. 16:49 ESV)

When we practice generosity in exile, we are doing a whole lot more than lending a helping hand. We are preserving our own souls and overthrowing the systemic mind-set that leads to exploitation of the poor. In small but significant ways, generosity is the powerful practice of breaking the vicious cycle of self-interest, freeing us to see ourselves in the faces of our neighbors. In practicing generosity, we remember our own poverty before God and his gracious and abundant provision of mercy, which we didn't earn or work to obtain.

God has been generous with us, and when we practice generosity, we testify that the chains of greed and overconsumption have been broken by the power of Jesus. Generosity is a revolution of grace. Once we have truly experienced the generous grace of God, we will graciously extend generosity to others.

Have We Really Experienced Grace?

The sad reality is that God's people in the United States are not very generous. *Christianity Today* interviewed several authors, inviting them to speak to the fact that Christians in 2011 gave just 2.43 percent of their income to charities. Ron Sider, author of *Rich Christians in an Age of Hunger*, had this to say:

> For Christians in the richest nation in history to be giving only 2.43 percent of their income to their churches is not just stinginess, it is biblical disobedience—blatant sin. We have become so seduced by the pervasive consumerism and materialism of our culture that we hardly notice the ghastly disjunction between our incredible wealth and the agonizing poverty in the world. Over the last 40 years, American Christians (as we have grown progressively richer) have given a smaller and smaller percent of our growing income to the ministries of our churches. Such behavior flatly contradicts what the Bible teaches about God, justice, and wealth. We should be giving not 2.4 percent but 10 percent, 15 percent, even 25 to 35 percent or more to kingdom work. Most of us could give 20 percent and not be close to poverty.[1]

We seem to be suffering from the same amnesia about which God warned Israel. We are so taken with the abundance of things to spend our money on that we worry we will miss out on something if we give our money away. And though we tell ourselves we don't approve of oppressive labor conditions, if we can get those products cheaper because someone somewhere worked like the Israelites in Egypt did to make it, we will more than likely buy those products to save a buck. You can see the fingerprints of Babylon smeared all over thinking like this.

When it comes to our money, we look a whole lot more like Babylon than we do the people of God. But it's never too late to let God set us free from endless wanting and selfish accumulation. God's dream for his people is that we would be an alternative community sustained by God even while we travel the aisles of a consumer culture that promises endless pleasure through endless products.

The transforming power of generosity ushers us into another story, a story in which as God's chosen people we use things and love people instead of using people and loving things.

The Bible doesn't recommend poverty in place of greed. Money is not the root of evil. The *love* of money is the problem. God calls us not to love money but to love God and others. Just as money can be used powerfully for evil, so it can also be used for good. When we taste the freedom that God gives us through the practice of generosity, we can become a powerful force displaying the generous kingdom of God. God's kingdom of generosity is better than the oppressive kingdoms of greed and consumption, and every human heart knows this somewhere deep down.

We become a living demonstration of the generosity of Christ when we practice his generous ways. Embedded in a world of endless anxiety as people strive to get more and pay less is a people waiting to burst forth in power declaring a better story. These people are the faithful presence of Jesus on earth and a prophetic witness to a better story.

To Bless

Generosity reflects the divine vision as we care for each other using our means to ensure that everyone eats tonight. When we experience generosity from another person, it radically and powerfully impacts us, because this type of gracious action is alien to the ways of life in Babylon.

The practice of generosity frees us from anxiety over scarcity and creates space inside us for acts of love. Exiles have a better story to tell, and freely sharing with others blesses the receiver and sets the giver free.

If you showed up at our church on any given Sunday, you would see large silver buckets set up at the communion table. Each one has an odd bumper sticker that says "Change for a Dollar." Change for a Dollar is an on-ramp to the practice of generosity. Every Sunday as a community, we each put a dollar in a bucket. The money is collected and set aside for anyone in the community who finds a need in our city that they sense God is calling them to meet. It is really a stretch to call this generosity because, honestly, a dollar is not a big sacrifice. We are not a rich congregation, but most of us can afford a buck.

The money is specifically designated for people outside our community. When God shows one of us a need, our entire community stand together to help meet it. A few times a month we hear stories of how people were able to demonstrate the generosity of God in the life of someone who found themselves in a place of need.

One woman told the story of a neighbor who was disabled and needed a wheelchair. For some reason, the system had failed to cover the cost, and the woman found herself housebound. Our church member was able to give her the money to cover the cost of the wheelchair in the name of Jesus.

Another story described a single mom who had been evicted from her apartment after her boyfriend had taken all of her resources and left her. A friend and coworker stepped in, and we were able to get her into an apartment with the first month's payment and deposit.

Hundreds of these stories, of people who were up against the harsh realities of scarcity, have passed through our church over the years. God, in his care, spoke into the hearts of his people, and gifts of hundreds of dollars were given to meet the needs.

Even though the situations are very different, the one thing that is the same in every story is the response. Men and women who receive a gift are drawn to tears, finding it hard to believe that someone cared enough to help meet their needs. For some, the generosity sparks an interest in faith. Others are left with the imprint of generosity on their lives from a generous God. The message is simple: a community in this city believes they have been rescued from their own poverty before God, and they are learning to practice his generosity.

All that for a dollar? That is the power of money in Babylon, but it is also the power of community. If each person were to practice generosity individually, their single dollar wouldn't make much of an impact, if any. But when we put our loaves and fish together, Jesus transforms them into a source of abundance that becomes a feast of joy for someone who is stuck in Babylon's wilderness.

When we as the people of God practice generosity in Babylon as a community, we can powerfully change the story of the purpose of money, revealing the power of love, which is so much stronger and more life-giving than the power of greed.

We call Change for a Dollar an on-ramp to generosity because it doesn't require much generosity to put a dollar in a bucket. After experiencing how much God can do with just a dollar, we begin to dream about what he might do if we were generous with our whole lives. What would happen, for example, if we collectively gave our time?

We have gotten a glimpse of this type of generosity as well. In Portland, a healthy partnership exists between churches and local schools. Over two hundred church and school partnerships exist.

Every summer before school starts, followers of Jesus from all over the city fill the school yards with rakes and shovels, truckloads of bark, thousands of backpacks and school supplies. During the month of August, almost every school in Portland experiences a makeover before the students return. We have served alongside principals and teachers who can't believe we keep showing up year after year. We have been able to work with the superintendent of schools in every district and various mayors throughout the years. Even Senator Ron Wyden has shown up to shovel a little bark with us.

The first year we collectively served the schools as the broader faith community in Portland was 2008. Over twenty-five thousand volunteers showed up to serve public schools. Sam Adams, who was mayor of Portland at that time, called it the greatest volunteer effort in the history of Portland.

Portland is not the most religious city by a long shot. The civic leaders who first partnered with local churches drew lots of flak from the broader Portland community. Suspicious people wrote and called to warn that this was all a ploy to proselytize their children. But school was not in session, and we serve without an agenda. We serve because our God has served us in Christ and called us to extend his generosity to the world.

I remember asking a city commissioner why he keeps partnering with us, given all the negative reactions he receives. He told me, "You are the only group that keeps showing up year after year, and your volunteers save the district well over a million dollars. Honestly, we can't afford not to partner with you."

Whether through a dollar in a bucket or four hours on a Saturday pulling weeds and painting walls, when we practice generosity, we bless the world as the faithful presence of Christ in our communities.

To Resist

When we practice generosity, we also resist the false narrative that our money and our time are our gods. We get to announce that giving is better than receiving and that when we give our lives away, we create more life in the world.

Through the practice of generosity, we announce that people are sacred and are not to be used or exploited but loved and served. We announce that money is a gift that can be shared instead of a master to be served. Generosity is a prophetic practice in that it reverses the rules of Babylon and critiques its false curse upon those who have landed on hard times.

We are often overwhelmed when we realize that we have been assimilated into the attitudes and values of Babylon in regard to our money. Even if we are opposed to selfish consumption, we have to admit that wanting more is something we struggle with.

There is a way to freedom, however, and it is through the practice of generosity. We don't have to figure out how to fix the systemic issues of an empire whose corporations are too big to fail. We are not called to fix Babylon; we are called to resist it and to be a prophetic witness in the midst of it.

The Three Parts of Generosity

The simple way forward is found in three words: remember, repent, and practice.

Remember

We remember that we all stand poor before God. Every bit of mercy, grace, and new life that we have experienced was unearned and undeserved. We were enslaved to sin and maybe enslaved to money, but we were not without hope, because God is a generous God. We are called to remember that Jesus took on our poverty in full. He gave up all his wealth to become what we are so that he could make us what he is. He became poor so that he could make many rich. We remember that we have received abundant generosity from Jesus and are still in need of it daily.

Repent

Repentance means to turn around. Jesus welcomes us to repent and admit that we have bought into Babylon's ways. We admit that the story we have been shaped by has come to an end. We are closing the book on it, and we are opening up a new book with a better story. Repentance is confessing that we are God's children, not citizens of Babylon, and that we are ready to put his generosity on display.

Practice

The best way to ensure that we have repented is to practice generosity. We don't have to make a big demonstration, but we should feel some effect in our bank accounts and on our calendars. God wants us to be generous with both our time and our money. People who live congruently in all aspects of their lives experience true, whole-life transformation. Jesus didn't save our souls to the exclusion of our checkbooks.

Practicing generosity opens up creative ways to give money that we have set aside as an act of worship toward our generous God. From tipping a waitress more to supporting a single mom with a small group of friends, we can find countless ways to practice generosity.

With each act, each dollar, each selfless expression of love, we bless those in Babylon and resist the Babylonian story in which we live. We bear witness that a generous God has a generous people living in exile. We declare that we are following our King, who saved us in our own poverty and set us free to enter into the poverty of others. Our God is not afraid of scarcity. He showers us with abundance, and together we put that abundance on display as we help the people in need whom we call neighbors and friends.

A revolution of generosity is breaking in through God's people. We are finding freedom from being enslaved to money. We are recognizing that we have enough and that there is enough to share. We are telling a different story of human purpose and the human condition. We are living as exiles in a country not our own, but we are free exiles, no longer carrying the chains of greed that once held us down.

Jesus practiced generosity to set us free to be a generous people.

ELEVEN

Sabbath

Sabbath may be the most important practice for the people of God, second only to hearing and obeying God's Word. Sabbath is the most peculiar of all the practices because it calls for something that is antithetical to the cultural demands to produce and consume. Yet the practice of Sabbath has the power to sustain and protect the identity of God's people in exile. Nothing seems to have the power to assimilate us into the values of Babylon like ceaselessly striving for more. In Babylon, we are trying to get ahead, but Sabbath is about getting off the treadmill of striving in order to retell ourselves God's story of who we are and whose world we are living in. Sabbath is the weekly rhythm that reconstitutes our shriveled-up energy with the living water of God.

Instituted at creation, Sabbath evolved throughout the generations of God's people. But one thing remained constant: Sabbath kept Israel more than Israel kept Sabbath. When they forgot Sabbath, they died, sometimes literally

but more often spiritually. Failing to keep Sabbath led to the loss of their identity, their distinctness, and eventually their home in the Promised Land. Scripture tells us that Sabbath breaking was one of the main reasons Israel went into exile:

> I said to their children in the wilderness, "Do not follow the statutes of your parents or keep their laws or defile yourselves with their idols. I am the LORD your God; follow my decrees and be careful to keep my laws. Keep my Sabbaths holy, that they may be a sign between us. Then you will know that I am the LORD your God."
>
> But the children rebelled against me: They did not follow my decrees, they were not careful to keep my laws, of which I said, "The person who obeys them will live by them," and they desecrated my Sabbaths. (Ezek. 20:18–21)

A Holy Time for Holy People

We are introduced to Sabbath within the first two chapters of God's story. God spent six days creating the world. On the seventh, he stopped and rested. God ceased from the work of creation, and while he called all of creation "good," the seventh day he called "holy." The holiness of the seventh day came from the fact that it was set apart. There was a pause in the rhythms of God's creation work. The pause was not simply the absence of work; the pause was also filled with the sound of its own rhythm. Sabbath was God's way of showing us that time has a beat that we are meant to dance to. We rest from work to get ourselves back from work that would otherwise reduce us to machines of production. Before sin entered the story, before work became cursed, there was still rest—holy rest for God's holy people.

This one-day rest shapes the way we understand the other six days. Work for the first humans could have seemed never-ending. There was much to do in the newly created world and not many people to do it. Similarly, we know there is always another project, another task, another email, another call to make. Work, as we have seen, has the power to reduce us to producers and consumers. Work, which is a holy calling, can easily become a drudgery we despise or an accomplishment we crave. Sabbath is the definitive word from God that defines the boundaries of work to protect us from being reduced to machines. Sabbath rest is holy because it is a day set apart from work so we can remember God is the one running the world, not us. There is freedom to enjoy our work, our relationships, and our God in Sabbath rest.

A single day carved out in which we cease from work seems like a simple thing, but once we try it, we quickly find that it is harder than it sounds. If we find it impossible to stop working and rest, to shut off our phones and not check our email, to spend an entire day being and not doing, then we are out of sync with God's creation rhythms.

Sabbath is a gift given to the people of God by a gracious Creator who reminds us weekly that we are not machines of production but sons and daughters cocreating with our Creator and helping humanity to flourish. It is a time for relationships, singing songs, and remembering who we are. In Jewish cultures today in which Sabbath is still seen as holy, the people work toward Sabbath rather than Sabbathing from work. For six days while they work, they are also preparing for Sabbath. Shopping for and preparing meals take place during the week. By organizing their schedules and making sure they get all their work done during the six days of work, they make Sabbath holy. They set it apart. They work toward it. When Friday night comes, they gather around the table and light a candle, welcoming Sabbath as they enter into holy rest.

In the same way, we as the people of God live into the rhythms of work and rest. Creating and ceasing become a way in which God forms us as distinct from the culture of ceaseless production. God's people dance to a different beat, and we show this as we live into God's rhythms of creation. Sabbath is a holy, life-giving experience distinct from the endless cycle of production and consumption.

The Impracticality of Sabbath

One of the primary complaints about Sabbath is that the idea of ceasing is not practical or possible in our cultural context. There is an expectation that we will live under the same regime of work and production as our neighbors. If we don't keep up, we get run over. This rule doesn't apply only to work. It applies to raising our kids as well.

When our four kids were younger, my wife and I counted how many miles she was driving getting our kids to all their events. She racked up over four hundred miles a week, and that was not counting the miles I drove.

How do we set aside a day for Sabbath when we are trying to fit in all of our kids' events? One child has baseball practice, another has a music lesson, another has a soccer game. Not to mention that the church keeps making us feel guilty for not getting our kids to youth group. The pressure is not easily relieved because Babylon would like us to believe that our children's entire futures could be jeopardized if they aren't participating in every event that is offered to them. If our daughter is not in year-round club volleyball, there is a good chance she will never play varsity in high school. In Babylon, no one is exempt from ceaseless striving.

The impracticality of keeping Sabbath and the potential effects of not keeping up with our neighbors cause many of us followers of Jesus to protest. Maybe we are taking this religious thing just a bit too far?

When we honestly assess our willingness or ability to keep Sabbath holy, we quickly confront the fact that when it comes to how we spend our time, we have been assimilated into the chaotic rhythms of Babylon. Sabbath is a shock to the system for people who have been caught up in such a pace of life as this. How does someone who has been living under the pressures and demands of contemporary American life suddenly switch gears?

New Freedom and New Life

The exiles in ancient Babylon recovered the practice of hearing and obeying God's Word. Gathering in small groups in synagogues, they were taught the stories of God's people from the Torah. As they listened to God's Word, they heard how God had powerfully saved his people from captivity. The primary text that would have brought courage to their hearts and faith to their souls told the story of God's deliverance of his people from the hand of Pharaoh. Exodus was the story that they recovered in exile.

Like most empires, Egypt was built by slave labor. Generations of Israelites had served at the mercy of Pharaoh's demands for more bricks. The people of God had become the brick makers of Egypt. This hellish existence continued day after day. Not unlike those experienced by American slaves, the conditions in Egypt were harsh and violent. People were property, reduced to human machinery for production.

After the Israelites endured four hundred years of slavery at the hand of the Egyptian empire, God heard their cries and sent a deliverer. Moses led a dramatic rescue that resulted in the emancipation of a community of slaves. Suddenly, generations of forced servitude were ended. The people of God were free. But in the days and years following their freedom, it became apparent that all those years of slavery had worn deep ruts in their hearts and souls. God had rescued them, but after generations of forced labor, freedom was a foreign experience. Their bodies were now free, but their heads and their hearts were imprinted by generational slavery. There had been no days off in Pharaoh's slave camps. The demands had never ceased. Violent retribution had awaited anyone who resisted. How would a community of slaves who had known only harsh and ceaseless labor learn an entirely new way of being?

Walter Brueggemann, in his book *Sabbath as Resistance*, put it this way:

> Pharaoh's system precludes and denies any such commanding voice that emancipates (v. 2). But YHWH persists: Let them go outside the system of restlessness that ends in violence. Let them depart the system of endless production, in order to enter a world of covenantal fidelity. In ancient context, they must depart from the Egyptian system in order to dance and sing freedom.[1]

God gave his people Sabbath to help them reclaim their identity as his free people. Sabbath was the powerful practice that God used to reorder the lives of former slaves. Hear the words of Moses from the book of Deuteronomy:

> Remember that you were slaves in Egypt and that the LORD your God brought you out of there with a mighty hand and an outstretched arm. Therefore the LORD your God has commanded you to observe the Sabbath day. (5:15)

The Genesis account of Sabbath taught them that they were to live according to the rhythms of God's created order. The Sabbath instruction in Deuteronomy taught them that Sabbath was the weekly declaration that they were no longer slaves but God's people who had been powerfully rescued from Pharaoh's forced labor.

God's instruction of Sabbath rest was the remedy that reoriented emancipated slaves and helped them to see the free rhythms of God's work-rest creation. The people were to remember that they had been slaves. They were to meditate on God's powerful act of salvation. Then they were to stop working and enter God's Sabbath rest. Even the simple act of gathering manna in the wilderness taught them about Sabbath. They were to gather enough for two days when they saw Sabbath coming. God was not a legalist. He was mercifully reforming his people, who had been deeply wounded by an imperial work program with its dehumanizing agenda. Sabbath was the practice that rehumanized them.

As the exiles in Babylon read these passages about the exodus and contemplated God's commands, they understood that life in Babylon, while not equal to the forced labor of

Egypt, shared the dehumanizing production agenda that turned humans into machines of consumption and production. Babylon reduced the holiness of work to an exercise of status and personal gain. Opportunity to get ahead was a great benefit of living in the empire, but getting ahead also turned neighbors into competitors and God-given gifts into assets for building wealth.

In the wilderness, God transformed former slaves into a community of neighborliness. In Babylon, the exiles learned that if they did not live out their alternative identity as God's Sabbath-keeping people, they would be assimilated by Babylon.

In modern-day Babylon, we are what we make of ourselves, but in God's family, we are because he made us so. Each person is a bearer of God's image and is worthy of being valued and loved. Sabbath is the practice that God continues to use to save his people from the forces of the empire.

The Transforming Power of Sabbath

When we protest that we couldn't possibly keep the Sabbath holy with the demands of modern life, we essentially mock the people of God who have come before us. Despite our technological advances, we are not that different from the slaves who were set free in the book of Exodus. Like them, we face the reality of being defined by what we do. We have the same well-worn ruts in our minds and hearts telling us that our ability to accomplish and keep up with the pack defines our value and worth. We face the same pressures faced by the exiles in Babylon. We too desire the good life that we see being lived by the wealthy among us. In essence, we share the same need. We need God to save us through the practice of Sabbath.

Sabbath is a practice of freedom for overworked people filled with anxiety and the fear of not having enough or being enough. Babylon wears us out. Jesus calls us into an alternative way of being in the world: "Come to me, all you who are weary and burdened, and I will give you rest" (Matt. 11:28).

The transforming power of Sabbath calls us to celebrate life just because we are participants in it. Sabbath is the weekly time when we can put our books down, turn our phones off, and shut our calendars so that we can feast and pray, play and take a nap. When we come out on the other side of Sabbath, we realize that the world has not fallen off its axis. The world keeps running because God is sustaining it, not us. The day after Sabbath, when all the work is there waiting for us, we come to it less weary, less burdened, and rested.

Soul rest is different from just taking a break. Spending an entire day bingeing on a TV show is a break from work but not necessarily soul rest. I don't want to get overly prescriptive, because we can turn Sabbath rest into a different kind of work, a religious work. But Sabbath is a time to get our lives back. I like what I once heard Eugene Peterson say about his Sabbath guidelines: pray and play. I think that's a good place to begin.

Sabbath is a time when all of the other practices can fold into each other in a meaningful way. Sabbath is a time when we can sit together and hear God's Word and discern together what obeying a particular promise or command might look like. It is a time when we can gather others around our table to show them hospitality, give gifts to one another in simple generosity, cease from work as we reflect on the fact that work is a sacred calling and that resting from it keeps our vocation holy.

If we are committed to practicing Sabbath, then all of the other practices tend to fall in line. Sabbath is the golden thread that God gives us to hold our faith together in a holistic way. When we practice it, we are transformed by it.

Sabbath Identity

As followers of Jesus, our fundamental identity is woven into the idea of Sabbath. Because we have been saved by grace, not by works (Eph. 2:8), we no longer need to strive for our acceptance by God. Grace has poured over us in Christ, and because Jesus took our sin and gave us his righteousness, we are freely accepted on the basis of his work, not ours.

The apostle Paul illustrates this new freedom in the contrast between how he describes his life in Romans 7 with the new reality of life in Jesus that he describes in Romans 8. In Romans 7:14, he laments that he can't do what he wants to do, because sin is right there trying to prevent him from obeying and pleasing God. In chapter 8, however, he rejoices that he is not condemned, because Jesus's work on the cross has set us free from sin and death.

The ramifications of this are that our very identity as God's people is a Sabbath identity; we are invited to stop working for God's acceptance and rest in the finished work of Jesus. Sabbath becomes all the more important for us who have entered into the rest of Christ's finished work, because by practicing Sabbath, we are also remembering that it is by grace we have been saved, not by works.

Sabbath as Faithful Presence and Prophetic Witness

When the people of God enter Sabbath rest, we simultaneously experience personal transformation and collectively bear witness to Babylon in a way that both blesses the culture and resists its relentless striving.

There is perhaps no more prophetic thing we can do in American society than cease from producing for twenty-four hours once a week. In a world of twenty-four-hour cycles and pressure to keep up our social media presence, disappearing for a whole day feels like treason to the way things are. But Sabbath is good news to those looking in from the outside. Babylon leaves everyone weary, not just the people of God. Anxiety over not having or being all that Babylon tells us we should have or be produces an exhausting existence. People are tired and their children are tired. The pressure is soul crushing. Sabbath-keeping people evangelize by keeping Sabbath holy. We share good news about our good God who has given us rest in Jesus. We don't need someone to graduate from college to have a party; we get to dance and sing and feast simply because God invites us into his Sabbath party once a week.

Everyone wants to get his or her self back. A cursory glance at self-help blogs and mindfulness practices tells us that people are thirsty and looking for a way to find refreshment for their souls. Sabbath is the announcement that God has given us a better way of being human. When we practice Sabbath, we invite our neighbors into the blessing of holy rest.

Sabbath is also a prophetic pushback on the dehumanizing practices of work and consumption. Hear Brueggemann again: "Sabbath is an arena in which to recognize that we live by gift and not by possession, that we are satisfied by relationships of attentive fidelity and not by amassing commodities."[2]

By practicing Sabbath, we agree with God that if we don't rest, then in our depletion we become objects of consumption and busyness, which is less than we were created to be. In essence, ceaseless work takes away the wholeness of our personhood, and we end up less than what we were created to be. Sabbath rest brings us back into wholeness and brings us into a place of trust in our relationship to God. We declare that being slaves in a market economy causes us to lose our agency to cocreate with God. Sabbath is the way we protest Babylon by announcing that there is a way to want less, need less, buy less, work less, and still be content and generous. Through Sabbath we can experience a fuller life because we are becoming more human each Sabbath day.

Sabbath is a radical practice of communal identity through which we prophetically announce that the people of God belong to God and have been rescued from the idols of wanting more and getting more. We confess that our God feeds us in the wilderness, and we will not live out of fear of scarcity. Sabbath is the physical demonstration of the spiritual reality that we are secure in the God who has saved us.

Don't Overcomplicate It

Practicing Sabbath shouldn't be overly complicated. We are stopping something in order to receive something. Calling it a practice helps us to be patient with ourselves, because getting it right is going to take time.

The first time I ever went snowboarding I refused to take a lesson. I was about twenty-two years old, I knew everything, and I didn't need anyone to help me. I got on the board, faced downhill, and began to pick up speed. Eventually, I could hardly breathe from the wind rushing against my face. Fearing I would run into a tree and die, I bailed hard against the packed snow. Frustrated and still unteachable, I unhooked the binding, walked up the hill, turned in my board, and headed for the café. I never learned to snowboard. A few years later, I told this story to a friend, somewhat ashamed of my attitude and embarrassed by my arrogance. He explained how to turn and stop with a few easy moves. All I had to do was not quit and get some pointers.

Practicing Sabbath can be the same type of experience. We shouldn't give up, and we may need some help to practice it well. In a rush to implement Sabbath, we may just turn everything off and announce to the kids that they won't be watching TV today. We should expect that isn't going to go well. Instead, we need to think through how to practice Sabbath and take the time to prepare for Sabbath.

As we begin practicing Sabbath, we should expect to grieve a little bit. We will miss working, checking email, playing with our phones. We need to give ourselves grace here. Over time, we will realize that we gain so much more than we give up.

So how do we practice Sabbath? Here are some ideas adapted from the website Sabbath Manifesto:

1. Avoid technology
2. Connect with loved ones
3. Get outside

4. Avoid commerce

5. Light a candle

6. Share a meal

7. Find silence

8. Care for the poor[3]

There are plenty of ways to practice Sabbath, and they are not one-size-fits-all activities. Sabbath is a gift, and we are just figuring out how to open it. As we give ourselves time, we will soon find ourselves anticipating Sabbath.

God created us to dance to the rhythms of his creation. Even in exile, we can find ways to live prophetically and faithfully through the gift of Sabbath.

TWELVE

Vocation

In 2015, ISIS beheaded twenty-one Coptic Christians. As the men kneeled before their executioners, they prayed to Jesus and confessed their faith. The video of their execution played out over the internet the following days and weeks. Many of us had heard the stories of martyrs, but few of us had seen people dying as martyrs in real time. "Martyr," for most of us, was a title reserved for the early Christians, but here were men dying for their faith in 2015. Terrorists live-streamed their so-called victory as the men fell to the ground and into the presence of the Lord.

Like many, I found the video difficult to watch. In fact, I turned it off before I saw them die. Struck by the ease of faith in my culture, I was embarrassed by my apathy. Each week at church we risk nothing but extra sleep to gather together and worship Jesus. While we gather, thousands of other Christians gather in the face of threats of death or imprisonment. If those threats existed here at home, I wonder who would show up for church. Would I cancel the service as I did when the snow was two inches deep on Portland streets this past winter?

I am always shocked by my own feebleness when it comes to faith. Being a pastor doesn't make someone a courageous witness for Jesus. I know this firsthand. Most Christians in Portland will tell you they are vegan or gluten-free or do CrossFit within minutes of starting a conversation, but we like to keep our faith private and personal. In modern-day Babylon, worshiping Jesus rather than the idols of our culture won't get us beheaded, but, sadly, most of us keep our faith a secret because we don't want to be found out. Not really the definition of courage, is it?

The video of the twenty-one martyrs brought to life for me the issue of vocation. Who are followers of Jesus called to be? What is our calling as the people of God?

Living faithfully in exile looks different in different places. When there is direct opposition to faith in Christ by governments and other religious groups, our calling to be unashamed and courageous is clear from the Scriptures. In a place like America, the opposition is subtler. America once held the values of Christendom, and as those values changed, so did people's attitudes toward faith in Jesus and Christianity as a whole. So we ask again, What does it mean to be the people of God now?

Faithfulness over Apathy

The practice of vocation is first and foremost a practice of calling. The word *vocation* comes from a root word meaning "to call." Vocation encompasses our entire life and primarily how we understand our purpose in the world and the contribution we are hoping to make.

When we think about our calling, the questions are many. What am I supposed to spend my life on? What will my contribution to the world be? How am I supposed to be faithful in the thousands of hours that I will spend working in this world? As we think about these questions, we need to ask an additional clarifying question: Is my calling connected to my faith?

More than likely we won't be killed for not bowing down to the gods of our culture, but that does not mean we shouldn't find a way to faithfully live out our calling in our time and place. If we aren't faithful to Jesus in Babylon, we will be assimilated by Babylon. In order to be faithful, we need to hear God's calling and obey it. The call of God upon our lives is a counter call to the callings of Babylon.

At the end of the day, our calling is to be faithful no matter what we face. That could be a terrorist who stands over us or an economic system that tells us the accumulation of money is the highest form of security we can have. Whatever moment we live in and whatever place on the map we call home, we as followers of Christ are called to trust in Jesus as our security and protection.

Members of the persecuted church don't have the luxury of apathy. For them, faith is a matter of life and death, and many choose life in Jesus even in the face of death. For too many of us in the West, our faith looks more like self-help therapy than authentic faith. Our faith is often about being nice and good and believing in a God who is a distant power who makes the world go well for us if we help ourselves and are nice to others. This is a Babylonian god who is comfortable with the empire's agenda and ready to help us fulfill that agenda. This false type of faith is pervasive in our moment in America. It invades our understanding of work, sex, money, and power. It also ensures that we end up assimilating the values and promises of Babylon. Christians who chase this type of faith will look less and less like exiles and more and more like Babylon itself.

The practices I am suggesting are meant to not only keep us in the story of God but also create a distinctiveness regarding what it means to follow Jesus in our time and place. Just like the practices of hospitality, generosity, and Sabbath, all tied together through hearing and obeying God's Word, pursuing our God-inspired vocation may feel costly but draws us deeply into worship and to witness.

What Work Is Not

To help us understand the broader sense of God's calling on our lives, we need to consider the story of the prodigal son, because in it we see a full picture of our calling as sons and daughters of the Father placed in this world to do holy work for a holy purpose.

Hear the story from Eugene Peterson's *Message*:

Then he said, "There was once a man who had two sons. The younger said to his father, 'Father, I want right now what's coming to me.'

"So the father divided the property between them. It wasn't long before the younger son packed his bags and left for a distant country. There, undisciplined and dissipated, he wasted everything he had. After he had gone through all his money, there was a bad famine all through that country and he began to hurt. He signed on with a citizen there who assigned him to his fields to slop the pigs. He was so hungry he would have eaten the corncobs in the pig slop, but no one would give him any.

"That brought him to his senses. He said, 'All those farm-hands working for my father sit down to three meals a day, and here I am starving to death. I'm going back to my father. I'll say to him, Father, I've sinned against God, I've sinned before you; I don't deserve to be called your son. Take me on as a hired hand.' He got right up and went home to his father.

"When he was still a long way off, his father saw him. His heart pounding, he ran out, embraced him, and kissed him. The son started his speech: 'Father, I've sinned against God, I've sinned before you; I don't deserve to be called your son ever again.'

"But the father wasn't listening. He was calling to the servants, 'Quick. Bring a clean set of clothes and dress him. Put the family ring on his finger and sandals on his feet. Then get a grain-fed heifer and roast it. We're going to feast! We're going to have a wonderful time! My son is here—given up for dead and now alive! Given up for lost and now found!' And they began to have a wonderful time.

"All this time his older son was out in the field. When the day's work was done, he came in. As he approached the house, he heard the music and dancing. Calling over one of the houseboys, he asked what was going on. He told him, 'Your brother came home. Your father has ordered a feast—barbecued beef!—because he has him home safe and sound.'

"The older brother stalked off in an angry sulk and refused to join in. His father came out and tried to talk to him, but he wouldn't listen. The son said, 'Look how many years

I've stayed here serving you, never giving you one moment of grief, but have you ever thrown a party for me and my friends? Then this son of yours who has thrown away your money on whores shows up and you go all out with a feast!'

"His father said, 'Son, you don't understand. You're with me all the time, and everything that is mine is yours—but this is a wonderful time, and we had to celebrate. This brother of yours was dead, and he's alive! He was lost, and he's found!'" (Luke 15:11–31)

Work as a Curse

For the younger son, work is a curse to be avoided. In a perfect world, he wouldn't have to work for a living. He could live the dream, inherit a fortune, and enjoy everything that Babylon has to offer. He is a young man with a wad of cash, ready to see the world and stake his claim.

This dream also fuels many of our lives. Developing an app that we can sell to Google so we can retire happily in our early thirties—now that's the American dream. Work is a means to an end, and the quicker we get to the end the better. Avoiding work while gaining its prize is a win-win. The word *prodigal* means "to spend wildly." We would all be prodigals if we could afford it.

When the younger son loses everything and has to work, it is misery. Work is always misery when we see it as a curse to be avoided. The good thing about the work is that it moves him closer to reality. He is not a god with unlimited resources; he is a son who has a father.

We too can learn something in the grind of hard work even when all we hope for is to escape it. Daily work with all of its pressures and pain has a purifying effect on the false beliefs we all have about life. We often believe that life would be better if we were independently wealthy and never had to work. We may look at the rich and famous and assume their life is full of ease. Work is hard, and by nature, most of us would rather get out of it. Who can't remember when they worked their first full eight-hour day? It lasted forever, and we felt we were missing out on all the great things our friends were doing while we were stuck at work. But the grind is not a bad place to be, because we begin to ask the deep questions about purpose and meaning and God.

Work is hard, but there is a redemptive place in the grind that can lead to awakening if we face it, put our shoulder to it, and learn from it. It can be a thing that you are stuck in for life and get by as best you can, or it can be understood as a sacred covenant that reflects God's union to his people through Christ. We can learn much that can ultimately lead us to God.

Work as an Identity Maker

For the elder son, work is a way to gain his father's approval and attention. Work is about his identity and position. The elder son has always worked, and he is a good worker. He is dependable, loyal, hardworking, and successful. He does what is expected of him. If we want to get ahead in Babylon, we have a better chance if we act like the elder son.

Many of us are elder sons. We despise those who get rich quick. We look down on others who don't share our work ethic. We have harsh words to say about those who don't put in the hard work. We got good grades, went to the right college, studied hard, and got a good job. We invested well and will retire with a nice party and a house to show for it. As with the elder son, work is proof of our value, our worth, our belonging.

Just like the younger son, the elder son has a twisted understanding of work. If the younger son thinks of work as a curse, the elder son sees work as an identity maker, a way to prove his personal worth. Both fail to see work as a part of their holy calling.

When we work like the younger and elder sons, we are fear driven and anxiety filled. The pressures we face in Babylon serve as a constant reminder that there is not enough, and if we only had enough, then we would be okay. Babylon tells us that we are not enough unless we produce enough.

First Calling: The Father's Love

Jesus's parable shows us that, as the people of God, we must first understand that we are called to come home to the Father. Before we are called to a career, a college, or a business venture, we are called to the Father's love.

Ironically, in Jesus's story, both of the sons are lost. One is lost in the wild world of pleasure. The other is lost somewhere in the backyard, working his way to acceptance and his father's approval. Both boys misunderstand the father's love. We also can't flee from our Father's love, and we can't earn it. The Father loves us, period.

The people of God in exile are called to be at home in the Father's love. He made us sons and daughters, and he celebrates over us. This is counterintuitive for those practiced in the ways of Babylon. God changes the rules of engagement.

We belong because we are his. We need to quit striving, because everything we need is found in the security of the Father's love. This means that our work will never have the power over us to create our identity. That has been secured by the Father. We are not a role, a title, or the job we do. We are children of God. Work is not our identity, and it's not a curse.

The people of God in exile are free to work in Babylon, but in a different way than Babylon intends for us to work. Work for us is a sacred participation with God in helping humanity flourish in a broken world. Work is holy because God put us in the world to help create a place where societies of people can become what God intends them to be. We are here to ensure that everyone has access and dignity and is empowered to contribute to the human project.

Sacred Calling to a Sacred Project

Many of us make a delineation between a vocation and a job. We mistakenly think that a vocation is a great career while a job is what the guy who picks up our trash does. This is a misconception of what vocation actually means. Vocation means we are participating with God in something he is doing in the world, as opposed to putting in the hours to get a paycheck.

Think about the last time you drove down the highway. What kept the other cars on their side of the road and prevented them from running into your car? The answer is something called a lane. At some point, someone somewhere decided that a road should contain stripes, white ones to separate people going in the same direction and yellow ones to separate people going in opposite directions. As a result, people can travel safely and orderly as they drive down the road. Take away the painted lines and watch what happens during rush hour. The person who drives the truck that paints the lines on roads doesn't have a mundane job. They are saving our lives, literally.

Think about what you bought at the grocery store recently. Where did the products come from? Who made them? Who grew them? Who picked the tomatoes and baked the bread? How did the milk appear in the carton? Who drove these things to your city? How did they get into the bins and onto the shelves?

Almost no job exists that does not lead to the flourishing of humanity. The jobs that don't lead to flourishing are criminal. Pimps and drug dealers, doctors who overprescribe opioids to make some extra cash—their activities do not make our communities and world better.

All noncriminal work is holy, meaning there are no mundane jobs. By thinking about our work this way, it protects us from turning work into an idol or drudgery. We as the people of God working as exiles in Babylon get to bless the people and the places where we work with the gifts we have been given that help another flourish. God wants this to happen. We get to participate with him in our work, not to get our identity from it or to figure out a way to get out of it but to show the world that work is holy.

The work of a pastor is no more holy than your work. We all work in a congregation of people loved by God, needing much grace and called to come home to the Father. The congregation may be in a church, a school, an office, or a factory. We go to work with people and work for people, and people matter to God. As followers of God, we work with an awareness that God wants all of his sons and daughters to come home, and he uses us in the places we work to invite them to do just that. We all work for the Father for his higher purposes, not simply a paycheck.

Sometime during this next week, someone will need to receive prayer from a pastor, nurture and discipline from a mother, a home to live in from a carpenter, life insurance from an insurance person, instruction from a teacher. Even in Babylon we are all interconnected and interdependent on one another. This is why God told the exiles through Jeremiah to pray for the city, because when it flourished, they flourished (Jer. 29:7). Where would we be without people who went to work every day to make the world work?

God at work with us is the center from which holy work is brought forth. We are sons and daughters loved by the Father and free to bless the world through our work.

Holy work takes a great amount of intentionality, but this practice of vocation, holy work as a rhythm of grace, is at once healing to our lives and prophetically inviting to the world around us. It is healing because it is grace-filled work and participation, not production and identity making. It is a prophetic witness because the world needs to see that work is not a curse to be avoided or an idol to serve. Both views lead to death, and something in our neighbors and coworkers knows this is true. We can be healed and be a witness simply by practicing the grace of vocation, holy work.

For some followers of Jesus, their vocation this week will be to courageously stand for Christ in the midst of violent aggression. For others, their vocation will be to faithfully keep painting stripes down the middle of the road, knowing that one day that kind of violence may be aimed at them. Either way, we are called to find our life and our security in our calling as God's sons and daughters, and we are free to give our lives away for the sake of others.

THIRTEEN

To Bless the City for the Sake of the King

At the end of our journey, I pray you are filled with hope. I believe that the past shows us that when the church has been marginalized or persecuted, it has been at its best. Being God's people now will require a more intentional faithfulness. With faithfulness will come the potential for the church in America to truly display the life-giving kingdom of God.

This is a time when the church has a great opportunity to be the people of God in a new way that will be a blessing to the world while ensuring that we don't lose the distinct identity we have been given as God's people, set apart. We may be aliens and strangers here on earth, but we are secure in Christ and already seated in heaven with him (Eph. 2:6).

Ours is an exile of hope, because our King has already conquered the greatest enemy, death, and overcome the world. As we wait for him to come in fullness and bring the fullness of his kingdom with him, we are not called to sit passively by. We are called to stand in faith, fight for faithfulness in prayer, and be ready to proclaim the hope that we have in Jesus. As we actively participate in the purposes of Christ, we are called to be bold in our faith, not shrinking back.

Practicing our faith through hearing and obeying the Word and Spirit, practicing generosity, vocation, hospitality, and Sabbath, we declare with our lives that another world exists, and we are experiencing the freedom it brings us, even now, through Jesus.

These practices may seem odd to our neighbors and friends, but I believe they will also be attractive to them. In a world like ours, people get tired and filled with stress—they are by nature hungry for hope. When we faithfully live for Jesus, more than likely we will be given opportunity to share with people why we live the way we do.

My prayer is that God's people will live in such a way that we regain a voice in the public square. As we live faithfully to Christ, may we use that voice to offer the beauty and life-giving message of Jesus in word and deed. I believe that when we graciously and thoughtfully carry this sacred message of Jesus Christ, the hope of the world, we will find ourselves in places of influence in our culture rather than in the margins of our culture.

And when we find ourselves in those influential spaces, we have an opportunity to shape the culture at large. I pray that you will steward it well, whether it is in city hall or the PTA at your local school.

My hope is that the gospel will become public truth and that God's people can become the type of citizens who live their faith winsomely in the public square. In a world of polarizing categories, followers of Jesus are the ones truly called by God to love and serve neighbors and enemies and to break through every barrier that seeks to separate us.

By living faithfully as the people of God, we are invited into an opportunity to work together with diverse groups of people for the common good of our communities, nation, and world.

There is no question that there are competing versions of reality among us, so how do people with these types of differences work together?

It has never seemed more apparent to me than it does today that we must move beyond the polarizing categories of winners and losers and the demonizing speech we use to speak about those we disagree with. If we care about working toward an alternative future, we will also need to find a way to go beyond simply agreeing to disagree, which becomes a way of suppressing our differences rather than embracing them as we embrace one another. The stakes are high right now. If we don't find another way of relating to one another, the most vulnerable among us will continue to be ignored.

As the people of God, we have an opportunity to imagine and create a new way in which citizens take part in public dialogues and inhabit public spaces with other groups of people for the common good of everyone who calls our communities home. We are called to seek the welfare of our communities. In a society filled with hate speech and social media contempt; in which religion, race, gender, sexuality, and politics have become dividing lines of exclusion; in which the church is equally at fault if not a more culpable participant, we need to find a new way of being human together. This moment may just be the time for that to happen.

The move I am suggesting is what Miroslav Volf called a move from exclusion to embrace.[1] What if we began to envision a nation in which we didn't simply tolerate our differences but engaged one another around those deeply held convictions? What if we moved beyond polite disagreement to demanding safety for those with whom we disagree and defending the rights of those who hold convictions other than our own? What if we truly believed that each of us bears the image of God and has something to offer the other? What new types of civility might emerge among us? This new kind of relating could create new possibilities of understanding, out of which relationships could be born and change could become tangible.

What if the people of God led the way in helping our communities become thriving human families whose civility made room for the embrace of one another as well as our differences?

These changes might sound like a long shot, but God's people living faithfully in exile can imagine and create a new way of living together in public space. With this kind of relational change, the most vulnerable among us have the best shot of finding security, hope, and opportunity.

We have a long way to go, and the road we travel is not an easy one. We face inequity, injustice lives among us, and too many voices have been unheard. Much needs to be acknowledged and made right. Living faithfully in exile won't put an end to our disagreements or dissolve our convictions, but doing so can reshape how those disagreements take place, who gets invited to the table, and how the challenges we face are addressed.

None of this is easily accomplished. But if the people of God live faithful lives, the dream of a civil society, a society of embrace and not of exclusion, is not as wild as it sounds. Civility can actually become a reality. When God tells us in Jeremiah to seek the welfare of the city, doing so is for our benefit as well as for that of the city. I dream of a time that I hope is not far off when our voices as God's people are turned to praise and not polarization and our energy and efforts are for building up, not tearing down. I dream that we will stand together when our moment has passed, and we will hear our King say, "Well done, my good and faithful one."

ACKNOWLEDGMENTS

I would like to thank the amazing people of Imago Dei Community. Your willingness to follow Jesus, take big risks, and continue to let Jesus change you encourages me beyond what I can say. The best days are ahead of us!

Thanks to Chad Allen, Alicia Cooper, and the good people at Baker who have been long-suffering with me through a challenging few years. Thanks for your understanding and concern.

Special thanks to Jack Kuhatschek. Your insights, push-back, and editorial expertise were beyond valuable to me. This book would not have taken shape without you, and for that I am grateful.

Thanks to Chris Ferebee for representing me and for your friendship over many years.

Thanks to the incredible staff members of Imago Dei Community, who continue to lead us into being a faithful presence and prophetic witness in Portland, Oregon. This is no easy task, and your persevering spirit and tireless work are a gift to Jesus and his people. Leading with you is a privilege.

Thanks to John Heintzman and Ben Sands. Your friendship, leadership, and accountability have made me a better man and leader. I am grateful for you both and excited for the journey ahead.

Thanks to the pastors and leaders in the Portland faith community. Your courage and faithfulness have made this an incredible moment to be a leader in Portland. Paul Roads has been a mentor on this journey—I am grateful for your faithful presence in my life.

Thanks to Jen Frankamp. You have served my family and me so faithfully over the last year. You are a true partner in the gospel. Your help getting this book to print has been enormous. I owe you a cheeseburger!

Thanks to my children Bryce Zach, Kaylee, Josh, and Dani. You have made the journey of life so rich for me, simply by being you.

Finally and forever, thanks to Jeanne. There are no more words to express the gift you are to me, my soul companion in the adventure of life, my greatest love and friend.

NOTES

Chapter 2 Where in the World Is Exile?

1. D. F. Morgan, "Captivity," in *The International Standard Bible Encyclopedia, Revised*, vol. 1, ed. G. W. Bromiley (Grand Rapids: Eerdmans, 1979), 613.

Chapter 3 Babylon

1. Babylon was the land of southern Mesopotamia. Politically, Babylonia refers to the ancient kingdoms that flourished in southern Mesopotamia, especially in the seventh and sixth centuries BC, whose capital city was Babylon (or *Bab-ilu*, meaning "gate of god"). The term can also be used geographically to designate an entire region (in present-day southeast Iraq). The adjective *Babylonian* has an even looser meaning; it may refer to the land or its inhabitants, to the kingdom or its subjects, or to a dialect of one of the principal ancient Mesopotamian languages. See W. A. Elwell and P. W. Comfort, eds., "Babylon, Babylonia," in *Tyndale Bible Dictionary* (Wheaton: Tyndale, 2001), 137.

Chapter 4 Baptize It, Burn It, or Bless It?

1. J. W. Gladwin, "Christendom," in *New Dictionary of Theology*, ed. Sinclair B. Ferguson, J. I. Packer, and David F. Wright (Downers Grove, IL: InterVarsity, 2000), 133.

2. Article C, section 175, "Position and Manner of Display," www.USflag.org /uscode36.html#175: "No other flag or pennant should be placed above or, if on the same level, to the right of the flag of the United States of America, except during church services conducted by naval chaplains at sea, when the church pennant may be flown above the flag during church services for the personnel of the Navy."

3. Gladwin, "Christendom," 133.

4. R. J. Mouw, *Abraham Kuyper: A Short and Personal Introduction* (Grand Rapids: Eerdmans, 2011), 114.

Chapter 5 Discerning Faithfulness in Exile

1. I heard Ravi Zacharias make this comment in 1994 while he was speaking at Reed College, Portland, Oregon.

Chapter 9 Hospitality

1. "Syrian Refugee Crisis: Facts, FAQs, and How to Help," World Vision, updated July 13, 2017, www.worldvision.org/refugees-news-stories/syria-refugee-crisis-war-facts#where.

Chapter 10 Generosity

1. Tim Stafford, "Ron Sider's Unsettling Crusade," *Christianity Today*, March 1, 2000, accessed March 15, 2018, http://www.christianitytoday.com/ct/2000/march web-only/12.0a.html. In this article Stafford quotes the following work: Ronald J. Sider, *Rich Christians in an Age of Hunger: Moving from Affluence to Generosity*, new ed. (Nashville: W Publishing Group, 1997).

Chapter 11 Sabbath

1. Walter Brueggemann, *Sabbath as Resistance* (Louisville: Westminster John Knox, 2014), Kindle, 18.
2. Brueggemann, *Sabbath as Resistance*, 85.
3. Sabbath Manifesto, accessed March 14, 2018, www.sabbathmanifesto.org.

Chapter 13 To Bless the City for the Sake of the King

1. Miroslav Volf, *Exclusion and Embrace* (Nashville: Abingdon, 1996).

Rick McKinley (DMin, Gordon-Conwell Theological Seminary) is the founder and lead pastor of Imago Dei Community. He is the author of four other books and serves on the faculty of Multnomah Biblical Seminary. Rick lives in Portland, Oregon, with his wife and four children.

Catch up with author
RICK MCKINLEY

▲ ▲ ▲

rickmckinley.net

@RickMcKinleypdx

PastorRickMcKinley

imagodeicommunity.com